BASICS
TEXTILE DESIGN
01

Josephine Steed
Frances Stevenson

sourcing ideas

D0492322

Fairchild Books
An imprint of Bloomsbury Publishing Plc

B L O O M S B U R Y
LONDON · NEW DELHI · NEW YORK · SYDNEY

Fairchild Books
An imprint of Bloomsbury
Publishing Plc

Imprint previously known as
AVA Publishing

50 Bedford Square
London
WC1B 3DP
UK

1385 Broadway
New York
NY 10018
USA

www.bloomsbury.com

**FAIRCHILD BOOKS, BLOOMSBURY and the Diana logo
are trademarks of Bloomsbury Publishing Plc**

First published in 2012 by AVA Publishing
Reprinted by Fairchild Books 2014

British Library Cataloguing-in-Publication Data
A catalogue record for this book is available from the
British Library.

ISBN PB: 978-2-9404-1163-4
    ePDF: 978-2-9404-4733-6

Library of Congress Cataloging-in-Publication Data
Steed, Josephine; Stevenson, Frances.
Basics Textile Design 01: Sourcing Ideas: Researching Colour,
Surface, Structure, Texture and Pattern /
Josephine Steed, Frances Stevenson. p. cm.
Includes bibliographical references and index.
ISBN: 9782940411634 (pbk. : alk. paper)
eISBN: 9782940447336
1.Textile design.2.Textile design--Study and teaching.3.Fashion
design--Study and teaching.
TS1475 .S744 2012

Design by Sandra Zellmer
Printed and bound in China

1
Floral patterns are the
mainstay of commercial
printed textile design.
Designer Aimie Bene
specializes in floral repeats,
where she uses Adobe
Photoshop to generate fresh
and dynamic print designs.

1

▼ **WHAT IS
TEXTILE DESIGN?**

▼ **RESEARCH FOR
TEXTILES**

▼ **THE TOOLKIT**

Headline
Chapter sub-headings are displayed at the top of each left-hand page.

Navigation
The current chapter sub-heading, as well as the one you have just come from and the one that you will be moving on to next are displayed at the top of the right-hand page.

Quote
Pertinent thoughts and words from well-known figures in the textile design world are displayed in purple boxes.

DRAWING TECHNIQUES **MIXED MEDIA** SCALE AND DIMENSIONS

144   MIXED MEDIA

145

The boundaries between design disciplines are becoming increasingly blurred. We see textile designers today working with many other types of materials. This offers new exciting possibilities and observational drawing techniques using mixed media are particularly useful in triggering new approaches to textiles.

Mixed media refers to the process of combining two or more types of media to create a single composition. This technique for observational drawing enables many different surfaces and textures to be made. Found objects can be used in combination with traditional drawing media, such as paints and pencils.

Mixed media extends the experience of drawing through the use of line, tone, texture, shape and form, using traditional materials together with other types of media such as collage, paint, paper structures and wire, investigating composition in two dimensions and in relief.

Some commonly used mixed-media techniques are outlined here.

COLLAGE

Collage is a technique used for assembling different types of materials together. A collage can include all sorts of materials, such as newspaper and magazine clippings, coloured and handmade papers, photographs, postcards and many other found objects.

Student collage work using a range of found paper collage materials. Collage gives this working drawing a range of patterns and surface effects that can then be used to develop further drawings and design work.

"Things have really moved on a lot. The materials I use range from wood and paper to plastics and metal.'
KAREN NICOL

COLLAGE EXERCISE

Gather together a range of found paper-based materials. These might include used envelopes and stamps, cardboard, old dress patterns, maps, newspaper, bus tickets or shopping receipts.

Using an A2 (C) sheet of paper, begin to assemble and glue your found objects whilst at the same time observing your composition (as for drawing techniques). Consider the shapes and forms of the objects and how they overlap. Rip, shred and cut paper edges to reflect the composition. This collage can then be further developed using traditional drawing materials to add detail and colour.

Introduction
Each chapter sub-heading is introduced by a short paragraph.

Excercise box
Exercises are provided to help the student to develop, evaluate and test their ideas.

Sub-head
Each chapter sub-heading
is broken down further
to allow information
to be easily accessed
and absorbed.

Caption
Each image is
accompanied by a caption
explaining the design or
ideas behind it.

10   11

RELIEF

Drawing in relief involves building up surfaces.
This can be achieved by creating raised areas
within a drawing through layering and overlapping
collage materials together. Consider using different
materials together, by layering tissue paper over
another surface, for example, the texture, print or
colour will appear through to the outer surface.

10
Student drawing using brown
paper and paint. The use of an
additional surface provides a
contrast in the depth and tone
of the colour to the drawing.

11
Student work using open
cut-work to create line patterns.
The effect of overlaying a number
of cut pieces gives the piece
additional depth.

OBSERVING LINES

Investigating line within your composition can
be done in a number of ways that don't always
involve 'drawing' on a flat surface. Drawing using a
sewing machine is one way of doing this. Wire can
also be used to investigate the three-dimensional
space. To do this, choose a pliable wire that can be
easily bent and twisted.

Try also cutting into paper with a scalpel to create
repetitive and patterned lines. This technique
changes the handle and quality of the paper where
it will begin to 'sag' or bend to create different
relief effects.

AUTHOR TIP

Here are some ways
to alter the quality of your
paper: folding, bending,
rolling, twisting, tearing,
crumpling, cutting, shredding,
puncturing, scoring, weaving,
layering, slotting, mushing.

Author tip box
Snippets of useful
information are displayed
in the form of author
tip boxes.

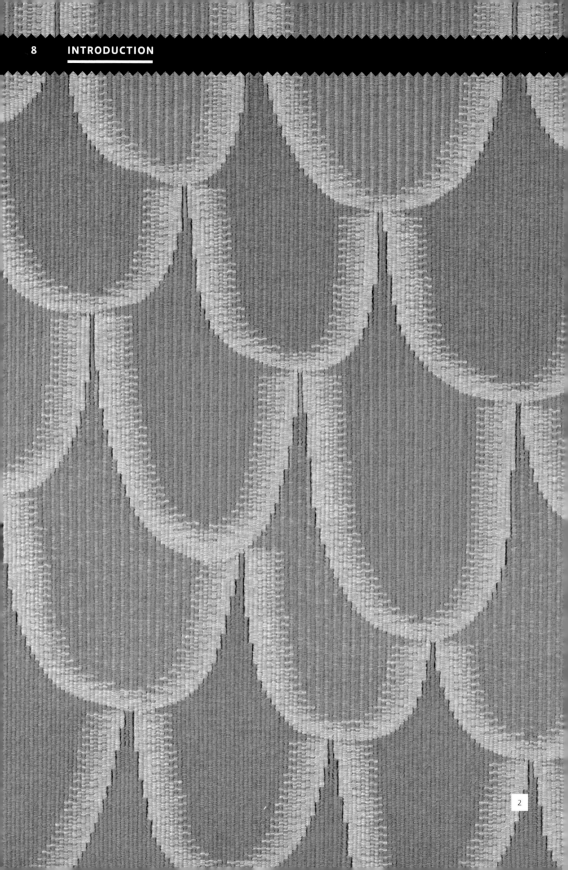

2

Textile design is an extensive subject that covers a wealth of design contexts, from wallpaper to clothing. Due to this breadth, textile design overlaps, links, and drives and innovates many other areas of design practice, including fashion, jewellery and architecture.

The creative journey – from concept to final design – always begins with a process of researching and gathering ideas. Many of the methods used to do this are similar to those used within other creative disciplines, but the textile designer views and analyzes the world around them through a very specific lens.

In order to produce inspirational textile outcomes, an understanding of the research and ideas–gathering stage is essential. This book aims to introduce the fundamental techniques required for this crucial part of the textile design process.

Throughout the book, visual examples and a number of short exercises help to fully equip the reader for their own creative experimentation. We hope you will find the book both informative and inspiring, as well as a helpful companion throughout your creative research and design practice.

2
This Tim Gresham tapestry shows a scallop pattern, with the textural qualities of weave structures and yarns adding to the richness of the fabric.

'I like to challenge
ways of looking at things.'
HANNA WEARING

1

WHAT IS TEXTILE DESIGN?

The research techniques used in textiles are similar to those used in other creative disciplines – fashion, graphics, jewellery and product design, for example. But when working with textiles, we need to explore the world around us through a different visual lens. To help us understand this, this chapter will look at textile design as a discipline and at how it differs from other creative subjects. We'll look at what textile designers do and why research is important to them. We'll look at the role of the designer and their responsibilities. Further on, we will explore the different occupations available to a graduate in textile design and find out what we mean when we talk about the textile industry today.

Overall, this chapter will introduce you to textile design and will demonstrate how textile research is ultimately personal to one's own creative interests and individual specialized areas of practice.

1
This garment from Manish Arora's collection demonstrates how textile design is such an integral part of the fashion industry. The print forms a dominant part of the overall piece and demonstrates the sourcing of motifs and the arrangement of colour and pattern. The overall composition is unique.

Textile design generally refers to the process of creating designs for knitted, woven, printed and mixed-media fabrics. The textile designer needs to be able to understand how to produce a design for a particular fabric type. In addition to this, they also need to be able to develop a textile design that is suitable for a given purpose – usually for the body, or for a particular space. Designers also require a good understanding of current trends, colour awareness and contemporary design issues, in order that their designs are up-to-date and relevant for their end purpose.

2
A student sketchbook showing an investigation into current knit designers. Awareness and understanding of what others are doing is an essential part of learning, as it gives insight into textile processes, techniques and contexts.

3
Textiles are used extensively in interior environments. Swatches of fabric are prepared in order to allow them to be touched and used for colour matching.

WHAT DOES A TEXTILE DESIGNER DO?   WHAT ARE THE OCCUPATIONS?

13

DEFINITIONS

A number of definitions can help to explain the main functions of a textile designer:

BODY   Used within the textile design industry, 'body' refers to fabric design for fashion, accessories and clothing, incorporating issues such as health, well-being and smart wearables.

SPACE   Textile design for 'space' incorporates textile and material design for the built environment, interiors, furnishings and transport.

Textile designers tend to specialize in either knit, weave, print or mixed media, where they can develop skills and knowledge specific to one of these areas. Each one of these specialisms requires a different type of technical knowledge, as well as different types of equipment and materials. They all encompass a broad range of design processes and approaches. Printed textile designers primarily work on the surface of the fabric. Woven and knitted (or 'constructed') textile designers tend to create a fabric from scratch, selecting fibres and yarns at the beginning of the process. Textile designers also often employ other techniques to create fabric (often referred to as mixed-media techniques). Mixed media is often used in conjunction with either knit, weave or print but is also a craft of making in its own right.

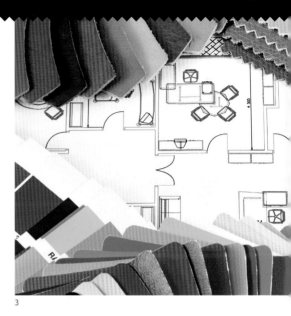

3

PRINT   A mark or impression made in or on a surface using pressure or chemical reaction.

KNITTING   Knitting, crochet or lace is created using yarn that interlocks, producing consecutive loops called stitches.

WOVEN TEXTILES   Fabric is made by interlacing the threads of the weft and the warp on a loom.

MIXED-MEDIA TEXTILES   Mixed-media textiles encompass many techniques, such as stitch and embroidery, pleating, bonding and felting, to name just a few.

For all specialist areas of textiles, designers start their design process with research. Research can take many forms but it is essentially the process of gathering, recording and analyzing information for developing into textiles. Research techniques can vary considerably depending on what type of designer you are. As a printed textile designer, you may perhaps be collecting information about surface, image, pattern and colour. As a constructed textile designer, you may be investigating structure, colour and pattern.

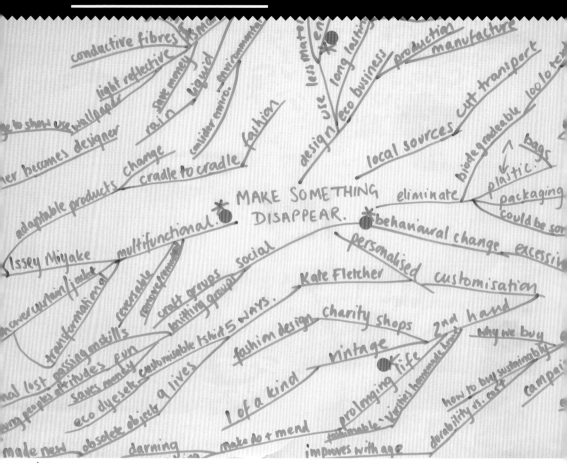

4

'Constantly evolving technology, innovation, art, design and traditional craft skills cohabit and fuse in the subject of textiles.'
ROYAL COLLEGE OF ART, LONDON, UK

WHAT IS THE ROLE OF
THE TEXTILE DESIGNER?

Textile designers have a wide range of roles and are often required to make decisions throughout the design process. For most, design practice begins with discussions with potential clients. Through presenting visual moodboards, portfolio work and verbal presentations, the designer discusses potential concepts and shows examples of previous design work in order to demonstrate their suitability for the project. This process is applicable to both freelance and in-house designers where they may have to pitch ideas to senior management within their design team and with their external clients. This also often involves trendforecasting themes and factors related to costs, sourcing materials, marketing and branding. In short, the role of the designer is multifaceted and design is only one aspect of their role.

Traditionally, the textile designer's major role was within colour, pattern and fabric aesthetics. This role is now evolving. Through the development of new technologies and social media, consumers and clients today can be involved in the design process from the start. Known as customization, the designer is not only designing but also working as a facilitator or co-participant with end users. The role of the textile designer becomes ever more complex and exciting.

WHAT RESPONSIBILITIES
DOES A TEXTILE DESIGNER HAVE?

Technological advances and changes in consumer lifestyles, together with sustainability and environmental issues, are increasingly becoming major factors for the designer to consider throughout the design process. An awareness of sustainability issues is imperative for designers. Designers are now required to consider where their materials originate from. Were they ethically sourced? Where did they come from? What processes were used in their production? Can waste be reduced? What is the lifecycle of the product and can it be recycled? What are the long-term implications of your design? Is it biodegradable? These are just some of the questions that textile designers are now being asked to consider.

Ethical and environmental considerations challenge designers in new ways. Many designers today recognize their responsibilities in reducing waste and their impact on the environment. Design companies are increasingly using their environmental and ethical policies as part of their marketing and branding strategies to encourage consumers to buy.

4
A student mind map exploring many of the issues relevant to society today. Mind maps are used by students at the start of their research process to help them define the context for their own work.

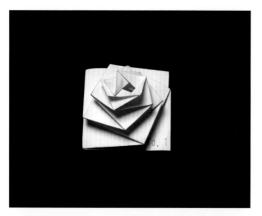

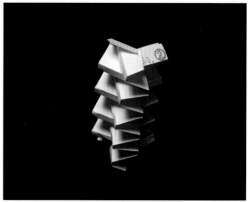

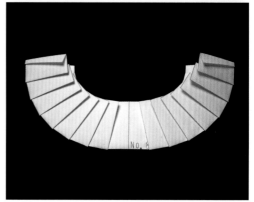

5

OBSERVATION AND AWARENESS EXERCISE

Take a look around you and note how textiles have been used in your environment. Consider the work that has gone into each stage of the process in order to arrive at the finished product you see now. Make a note also of all the ethical and sustainability considerations for each stage.

5
Japanese designer Issey Miyake has gained a reputation for pushing the boundaries of fabric experimentation. In his 132 5 collection, he creates a series of intricately folded polygons made from recycled PET (polyethylene terephthalate) which transform into clothing when placed on the body.

WHAT DOES A TEXTILE DESIGNER DO?   WHAT ARE THE OCCUPATIONS?

17

6
This 'exhaust' print by Becky
Earley demonstrates a more
environmental printing method,
involving minimal chemical usage.
Becky Earley is well known
for her commitment to sustainable
textiles and was one of the first
people to print onto fleece fabric
made from recycled plastic bottles.

Textile design education provides opportunities for a variety of different career paths. In the previous section, we mentioned the distinctive design and technical differences of knit, weave, print and mixed media. Following on from this, we will now look at some of the design professions available after specializing in textile design.

CRAFTSMAKER

Textile craft can be used to describe a wide range of textiles, including one-off, commissioned or limited-edition pieces. Craftsmakers often work alone but frequently exhibit collectively and pool resources by sharing communal studio spaces. They have a highly developed understanding of their particular niche market, developed over many years of refining their practice. Craft is such an expansive subject but can include makers working within the applied arts, textiles for exhibition, conceptual textiles, three-dimensional textiles, accessories and clothing. Major craft fairs are held annually across the UK, Europe and North America.

7
James Donald is a Scottish weaver who produces exquisite handmade woven textiles from his studio in Edinburgh. James produces textiles for both fashion and interiors.

8
Examples of handprinted and painted accessories by craft practitioner Frances Stevenson. Practitioners who print require enough space to house a print table plus an area to mix up dyes, and coat and expose their screens.

8

'Craft is an extraordinary thing of wonder; encompassing skill, creativity, artistry and emotion with thought, process, practicality and function. It is one of the purest forms of expression.'
TRICIA GUILD

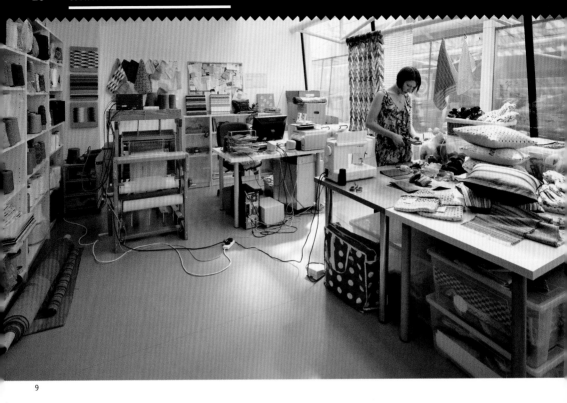

9

STUDIO DESIGNER

Working within a studio is undoubtedly the
preferred working environment for most designers.
The term studio immediately alludes to creativity
and experimentation, portraying a strong identity
of a particular designer or company. But there are
many different types of textile design studios.
Designers working within commercial design
agencies sell fabric or paper designs to a broad
range of potential clients, ranging from high-end
fashion houses to well-known high street brands.
Most fashion and interior companies also have
their own in-house design team. Many design
agencies will showcase their studio's designs at a
large trade fabric fair such as Indigo, which is part
of Première Vision, the world's largest clothing
fabric fair held in Paris twice a year.

9
Weave designer Angharad
McLaren in her studio. Working
in a studio is undoubtedly the
preferred career path for many
textile designers.

10
An enormous selection of yarns
can be purchased from shops
and yarn suppliers. Knit and weave
students need to learn about
yarns in order to understand how
they work together and how they
will react when 'finished' in the
washing-out process.

11
A yarn designer produces shade
cards for knitted and woven
textiles. Colour matching and
colour proportions are usually
worked out by wrapping yarns
onto cards such as these.

YARN DESIGNER

An often overlooked but essential area for textile design is of course yarns. These again need to be designed by yarn spinners in order to be applicable for a given fabric design and purpose. Often, the main focus for the design of yarn is colour (and the colour prediction industry plays a vital role here). However, yarn also includes a wide range of specialist yarns. These specialist yarns are often produced specifically for the knitting and weaving industry and also for the amateur textile market, such as hand–knitters and craft enthusiasts. Twice a year, the world's premier trade yarn and spinners' fair, Pitti Filati in Florence, Italy, enables yarn manufacturers to exhibit their yarn collections primarily to the knitting and weaving industry.

10

11

CAD/CAM DESIGNER

Computer-aided design and manufacture, also known as CAD/CAM, is now a large part of the textile industry. Textile designers increasingly work with CAD to produce their designs, which can then be reproduced on compatible computer-operated machinery. Many CAD agencies today employ textile designers to use digital technology as a creative tool to realize their design ideas. Design work can then be digitally transferred anywhere in the world to be manufactured. Individual textile designers are also using technology for a number of other purposes: such as to engage with their customers through social media networks and forums, through their own individual websites and through e-commerce websites for collective artists and designers.

12
Studio image of the Centre for Advanced Textiles (CAT) in Glasgow, UK, a design agency that specializes in digital printing for textiles. Design work is finalized on the computer and then transferred to the digital printer.

13 & 14
The design studio of Timorous Beasties, who are known for their surreal and provocative textiles and wallpapers. They are distinctive in that they use traditional flatbed screen-printing processes. Their large print table can be seen in the photograph facing.

12

13

'Technology is making design more exciting, with colour, wallpaper, textures, fabrics that could never have been created without the technology.'
DAVID BROMSTAD

15

15
Fashion forecasting is used in the textile industry to create concepts for the fashion and interiors markets. Companies rely on this information in order to direct their future collections.

16
A student sketchbook that shows collected information relating to colour analysis. Students look at prediction companies for information regarding colour analysis, particularly if they intend to work in the textiles industry after graduating.

Zinnias

Ff

PA 101445

16

FASHION FORECASTER

Fashion forecasting companies primarily provide the fashion and textile industry with information on proposed key styles and looks for the future. They usually work two to three years in advance. This timeframe is vital in order to supply the textile and fashion industry, from yarn manufacturers to high–street retailers, with the themes, colours and styles to work on for the coming seasons. Textile designers are well equipped to work within this creative environment. Often, designers are asked to produce fabrics on a given theme or to work directly on collating information on future trends.

COLOUR PREDICTOR

Colour prediction is closely related to fashion forecasting and the two often go hand in hand. Colour is an essential element of fashion and textile design, and getting it right is a highly specialized job. More and more industries are today using colour prediction information as design becomes the main focus for consumers. The design of our mobile phones, computers, the cars we drive, and even the layout and colours used within shopping centres are all carefully considered using colour analysis and prediction data.

THE TEXTILE INDUSTRY

When using the term 'textile industry' we are usually referring to the commercial manufacturing side of textiles. The term also incorporates all the subsidiary businesses working together within clothing and fabric manufacture. These include spinners, dyers, fabric finishers, trimmings manufacturers and accessory producers – essentially all those providing a service or product for textile companies. As a textile designer, you may work as a commercial designer for a large manufacturer or as a freelance designer commissioned to design a range for a particular company or brand. Whatever area of textiles you ultimately choose to work within, you will need to have an understanding of how the textile industry operates. Many textile courses today have well-established links with textile companies. Student projects and placements are perfect for gaining experience within the industry, and can often lead to further design work or job offers.

17
Jobs in the textile industry can include spinners, dyers, fabric finishers, trimmings and accessory producers. An understanding of the textile industry is essential for all textile designers.

17

Reiko Sudo is one of the founding members of NUNO Corporation, an innovative textiles company based in Tokyo, Japan. Sudo's textiles are known for their combination of traditional techniques and experimental effects. Her work has revolutionized textiles within interiors, fashion and art, and has been shown all over the world, including in exhibitions at MoMA, New York, USA, the Museum of Fine Arts in Boston, USA and the Victoria & Albert Museum in the UK.

▶ **18**
PLEATED POLYESTER WITH STAINLESS STEEL FINISH

This fabric comes from Sudo's 'Metallic' series, where fabrics were woven with fine threads of alternative materials.

▶ **19**
JELLYFISH FABRIC

To create this textile, an industrial vinyl polychloride fabric was partially affixed onto a polyester organdie in a checkerboard pattern. The fabric was then subjected to a flash-heat treatment, which caused the polyester organdie to shrivel where adhered. As the fabric is thermoplastic, it retains these crinkles even after the vinyl polychloride is peeled away.

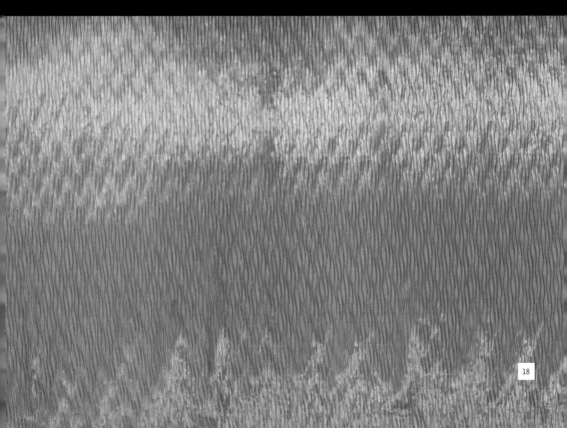

18

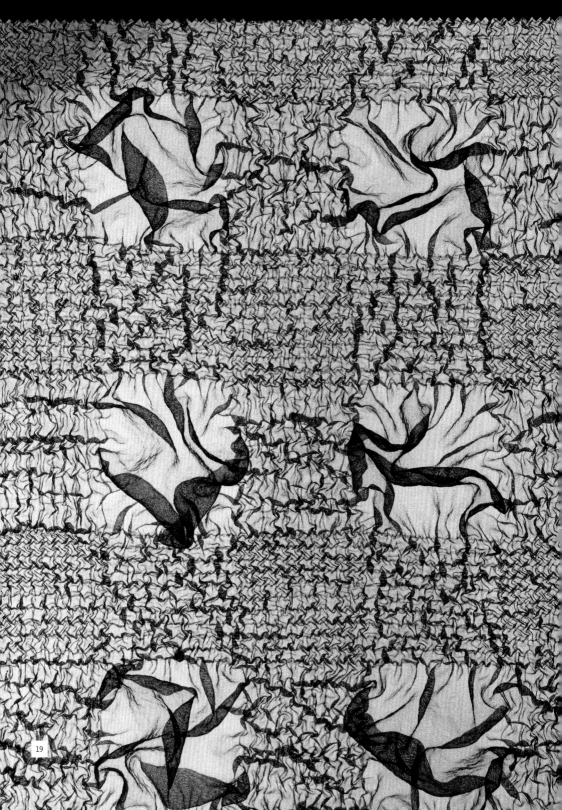

19

Donna Wilson designs and makes accessories and products for the home. Everything stems from the soft knitted creatures she started making while at the Royal College of Art, in London. These misshapen, odd creatures are inspired by everyday oddities and peculiarities of life. They are loosely based on the characteristics of Wilson's friends and the beautiful naivety of childhood drawings. The ever-growing collection now includes furniture and ceramics which are proudly made within the UK, and Donna is passionate about British manufacturing and craft skills.

HOW DID YOU GET STARTED?

I graduated with a degree in textile design and then got a job in a knitwear company as an assistant designer for a year. I then went back to college to do an MA at the Royal College of Art in London, where I specialized in Mixed Media Textiles. While at college, I started making products and sold them in design shops in London. They started off as long leggy dolls, which were unique dolls made from recycled jumpers with bright sheep's fleece hair. They soon evolved into less conventional knitted creatures with two heads or extra long legs, each with their very own character. The more peculiar the better for me! I launched my business in 2003 with a single knitting machine, producing and selling designs in tiny numbers.

WHERE DO YOU WORK?

I work in my studio in East London with my team of four to eight people, and four outworkers, from Bournemouth in southern England to Orkney in Scotland.

WHAT IS THE ENVIRONMENT LIKE IN YOUR STUDIO?

The studio is bulging at the seams with cones of rainbow-coloured yarns, bits of wool and felt, knitting machines and odd creatures! It's all a bit unorganized and untidy but I seem to work better like that. I like listening to music, which I think makes the atmosphere a bit more fun and connects me to the outside world. Natural light is very important to me as I need to be able to get colours exactly right.

20

20
Donna Wilson in her studio.

21
A selection of Donna Wilson's knitted products from her studio.

22
Donna Wilson quirky knitted gloves.

21

CAN YOU TELL ME ABOUT YOUR DESIGN PROCESS? HOW DO YOU GENERATE IDEAS?

I usually start with sketches in a notebook. They look like little cartoons with tiny bodies and huge exaggerated heads. I work on paper first to get the look of my designs to work and then start knitting. Usually, they turn out very much like the drawings but occasionally I'll make some out of the scraps or offcuts. Sometimes, these rejects are just as successful as the planned ones. When designing the larger furniture pieces, I have been known to make models out of plasticine, as my technical drawing skills need work!

WHERE DO YOU START YOUR RESEARCH?

Sometimes I start by collecting things I like. I always keep my eyes open for interesting designs or imagery. I also work a lot with the materials in a very hands-on way so sometimes ideas come from that. I try to look around the shops a lot and also through style magazines, which I think is important.

CAN YOU DESCRIBE YOUR DESIGN PROCESS FROM START TO FINISH?

I tend not to be too structured. For me it's a fairly spontaneous process. I suppose the structured way would be to start with visual research, collecting inspiring imagery, making a moodboard of ideas, sampling with materials, doing sketches, more sampling, making adjustments to get the finish right. I'm working more on the computer now just because it's a quicker way to generate designs, but it's important to keep drawing too. I also think about the different ways to produce a design. For example, is the piece a handmade one-off piece, can it be made by machine, do I need to source an outside manufacturer?

WHAT INSPIRES YOU?

I love the Scandinavian aesthetic and the Scottish landscape where I grew up. I'm inspired by my surroundings. I was brought up on a farm in Scotland. This has influenced the way I like to use textures, colours and form. My early work was all about the shades and textures of rural landscape.

WHAT OR WHO HAS HAD THE MOST INFLUENCE ON YOUR WORK?

An early influence was Alexander Girard, the late Italian–American textile designer. I like his colours and prints, also the fact that he too worked in different media.

I love Julie Arkel's little people and I'm also inspired by documentaries I've seen about Siamese twins and people with gigantism.

My childhood spent in the countryside has been a continuing strong influence in my work where my love of tactile qualities originates. The vast landscape and roughness has had a strong influence on my need for textural and organic forms.

WHAT IS YOUR GREATEST ACHIEVEMENT TO DATE?

It would have to be winning *Elle Decoration* magazine's British Designer of the Year Award for 2010!

22

ower blocks and modernist buildings are not often viewed with affection, which makes it all the more surprising to see how appealing they can look
used as decoration on
me to think of
of
displaying my work.
and mugs are decorated with line drawings of vibrantly coloured plates buildings by the likes of Erno Goldfinger and Peter and Alison Smithson. Their collection also includes notebooks and tea towels, and they will create pieces to order (from £6; www.peoplewillalwaysneedplates.co.uk).
Ella Doran uses photographs of details of everyday objects as prints for tableware and textiles. Her humorous Brick Wall blind is a play on a city dweller's "view" of another building (from £150, to order; www.elladoran.co.uk).
For spring, Habitat has employed Nigel Peake to perk up its picnicware with his urban-inspired drawings scrawled across a range of melamine platters, beakers and trays (left, £15). Having spent six years studying architecture,
alents to illustration, but references his building background in his work. "I am
tectural things, but without them being directly architecture," he says. "For this
out 80 to 100 buildings – inspired by Shanghai and New York – then collaged
ake each design 'site specific' to the object it was for."
ly built-up world, beautifying street life is recognition of the way we live now –
tion of it.
NEW BUILDS
1 We do love a cheap'n'cheerful accessory that lets you try out a trend. This Sainsbury's Cityscape mug fits the bill.
2 The artist Sharon Elphick prints her photographic montages of buildings on canvas, Perspex or glass. Technicolour Towers; www.sharonelphick.com
3 Alice Mara seals photographic transfers of buildings she likes onto plates, bowls and cups. The images complement the form of the vessel and vice versa. Building oval dish; www.alicemara.com
It's always nice to have a good "stuff" shop on your doorstep, and Horsfall & Wright is my local homes "stuff" shop. Among its many well-sourced pieces is a range of linen cushions, embroidered with images of some of London's best-loved buildings, by Snowden Flood. Tower Bridge cushion; www.horsfallandwright.co.uk
1 £2
2 £790
3 £350
4 £60
Childrens Clothing 'PWANP'
Nigel Peake
'People Will Always Need Plates'
1

2

RESEARCH FOR TEXTILES

Research for textile design engages the student with the contexts for textiles themselves and the uses and functions that textiles have. It includes exploring the aesthetic qualities of textiles – the visual and tactile world of colours, textures, surfaces, structures and patterns – and it involves looking at how cloth or textile materials are used. This might be wearable textiles, textiles in the domestic environment, textiles in a commercial or industrial environment, or new materials that break boundaries in areas such as science and electronics.

In order to design textiles, students must develop the ability to engage with the world around them and be able to see things that might lend themselves to a textile outcome for an identified purpose. This involves being receptive to the world in a visual, sensory and critical way in order to be able to analyze and synthesize aspects of the environment.

1
A student sketchbook, showing how ideas can be collected and analyzed. These can come from a range of sources – from architecture to graphic design.

There is no specific answer to this question, except to say everything and anything! Textile designers, like all designers, are curious about the world that surrounds them. They are seekers of new ideas and are hungry for creative inspiration that will inspire innovative products or ideas that they believe might be useful, practical, beautiful or inspirational for people to use and live with.

WHERE TO LOOK FOR INSPIRATION

Historically renowned textile designers like William Morris famously gathered their visual inspiration from nature. Morris used nature's ingredients to formulate the natural dyes that he used to print cloth and dye yarn for weaving. He revived the industrial use of the plant–based indigo dye made from woad, which is prevalent in most of his work. Researching textile techniques (like dyeing) through contemporary or historical contexts remains an essential part of a textile designer's development process, as this can fuel the direction of their work.

Our environments vary across cultures and over time. This is what makes each designer different, as plant and natural forms, colours and light, architectural forms and materials and so on vary in every part of the world. Textile designers also explore the contexts for textiles and how textiles are used in order to reflect on what is current, contemporary and relevant to us within our own spheres.

Textile designers today look to their own 'natural environments', which includes the urban as well as the rural landscape. Different things inspire them and they see and respond to their surroundings in various ways. They translate and record the world visually and experientially in order to use this information as the source for design development. This normally includes experiencing colour, shapes, forms, structures or textures, which act as a constant source of inspiration.

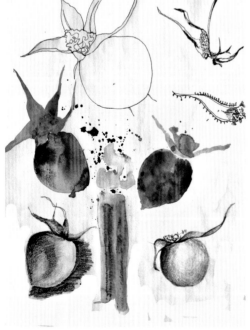

2
Student worksheet, with detailed observational drawing (primary research) of plants using various techniques. It is a good idea to look thoroughly at your source, and examinine it from different angles.

3

4

5

6

3
A student's mixed media collage, taken from still life sources (primary research).

4
A selection of magazines (secondary research), allows you to investigate what designers are doing in different areas.

5
A student sketchbook page, containing observational drawings of architecture using mixed media techniques (primary research).

6
A student sketchbook page, showing representations of plant forms (primary research) created using paint, collage and pen.

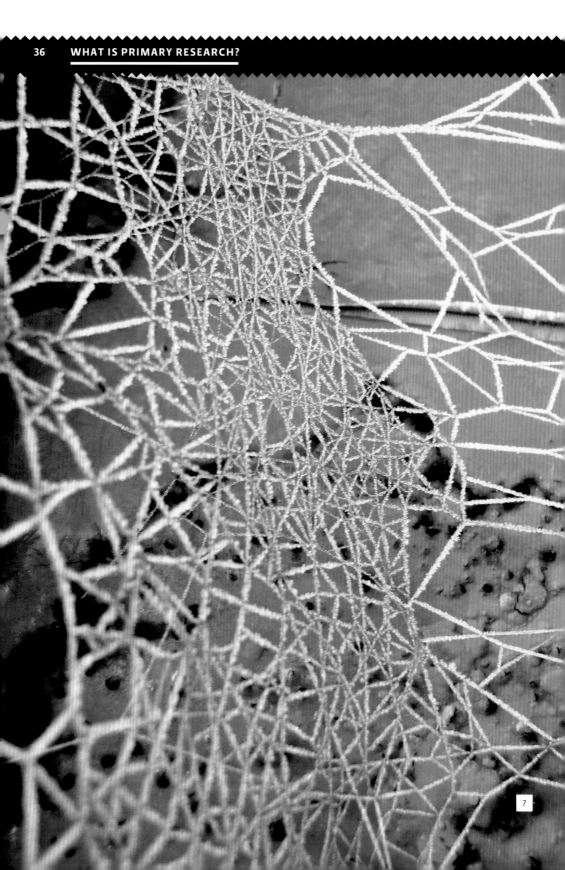

WHAT DO DESIGNERS RESEARCH?   **WHAT IS PRIMARY RESEARCH?**   WHAT IS SECONDARY RESEARCH?

37

This type of research refers to objects, places or situations that you find and experience yourself in. Something that you see, hear or touch for example; something that is 'unearthed' by you. As a textile designer, this information might be found on a research trip where you record what you are seeing and experiencing through drawing, painting, mark making or photography. The journey itself may become part of your research as well as the destination. Primary research is a direct type of research that involves all your senses in response to your surroundings, but it must also include your knowledge and understanding of textile contexts, since you should have an awareness of what you are collecting information for.

Primary research also includes having conversations or interviews with other people. Listening to someone tell a story, for example, may conjure up moods and colours or textures and feelings. These may relate to something that you have had experience of yourself. Primary research may also include festivals or carnivals that you attend and experience which may evoke moods of humour, exuberance, sobriety or decadence that you may wish to adopt in your work.

Therefore, primary research is the essential ingredient for all textile design research as it provides the main drive for the designer. Quite simply, it is the excitement of the primary research that makes the designer want to design.

TYPES OF PRIMARY RESEARCH

Textile designers collect things that they see and touch. If possible, they often collect their sources in order to refer back to them as they work. This achieves three things: it provides them with a visual source with which they can examine colour and texture, and so on. It also provides them with something they can physically hold, (it may be the coolness, roughness, smoothness or weight of the 'source' that inspired them). And having the source (which may be an object) to hand helps to bring back the feelings and experiences of that day. This is important, as it is the sensory experiences that can influence the designer in how they begin to translate and develop their ideas.

7
Photography is an excellent way to capture a piece of visual information that may not be there for very long. This web is extremely fragile but the structure, colours and patterns have been successfully recorded for future reference.

AUTHOR TIP

Make sure that you have a good collection of drawing materials with you. It's a good idea to make a portable toolkit using a small toolbox that has a range of different media and papers. Also have a small sketchbook with you to quickly make sketches, write down notes and ideas and to collect things which might interest you.

8

VISUAL RESEARCH

Visual research involves looking at things closely. This may sound easy, but it is much harder than you think as it relies on your being open to what you are seeing in a whole sense and allowing yourself to relax and respond to the visual stimuli. For example, being in a busy noisy street on a dark cloudy day, surrounded by modern architecture, may require the designer to work and respond in a fast-paced way, drawing with bold marks and using urban colours that reflect the pace and movement of the street. Your whole body should respond to the emotions and physicality of the situation, so that this will be reflected in your work.

You can also focus in on aspects of your situation. For example, if we think of a busy street, there may be a dark, leafless and forbidding tree standing defiant in the midst of the chaos. You may decide that this is your focus and set out to capture the strength, scale and loneliness of the tree in its urban landscape. You should carefully select drawing materials that will help to reflect the mood of the scene – thick black charcoal might work, for example, giving high-contrast effects.

You may also be looking at the tree and thinking metaphorically; the tree is rooted in this place, and is growing and branching with the businesses of the location. Or, you may be interested in the patterns of the branches or the textures of

WHAT DO DESIGNERS RESEARCH?   **WHAT IS PRIMARY RESEARCH?**   WHAT IS SECONDARY RESEARCH?

39

9

the bark. Whatever aspect you hone in on, the wholeness of the situation still applies.

Visual research is crucial to every designer and it is important to learn to be curious about what you are looking at so that there is a continuous driving passion for design development.

8
A student drawing, created using ink and bleach to capture texture. Try to ensure that you choose a medium that will recreate the mood of your source.

9
A student's 'quick sketch' of a street scene. Sometimes, a situation requires us to work quickly. This can be very effective as we can still get a good sense of pattern and motif, and this can be developed further away from the scene.

OBSERVATION TECHNIQUES

Always try to remember that you are gathering information that you can use to develop into textile designs. You are not necessarily drawing 'a picture' in the traditional sense. It is important to think of your research as 'information gathering' at all times, as it is the first, and most crucial stage of your research process.

It may help to consider your page as a worksheet where you can record forms, shapes, interesting surfaces, patterns or colours. You may also have to try and think differently about how you are looking. Try zooming in to see close up, or try looking at something via a mirror just to see it in a different way. Look at things from different angles or take photographs and then examine them. Use your imagination at this stage in order to see potential in the everyday.

Think of yourself as an explorer observing something for the first time. Look in places that are familiar to you but where you might not have looked previously. When you stop and take time to observe, you will begin to see subtle changes in colour on what appears to be a white wall, or a variation in form on each leaf on that tree or a pattern emerging through the sunlit shadows of venetian blinds.

It is a textile designer's ability to seek out design potential from everyday surroundings that makes them special.

10
Try and collect different papers and textures to use in mixed–media pieces as part of your research process. This student's collage uses old music sheets, newspapers, textured paper, wallpaper, tissue paper and petals.

'I can study an insect forever, noticing the gossamer textures of their wings and the soft fibres that cover their shells.'
KAHORI MAKI

WHAT DO DESIGNERS RESEARCH?   **WHAT IS PRIMARY RESEARCH?**   WHAT IS SECONDARY RESEARCH?

41

11
A student's observational drawing, made using black ink and felt pen. The black–and–white drawing gives a very high-contrast image which is ideal for developing pattern structures.

12
This student study uses cream coloured paper, which gives a much softer tonal effect. Remember to think about the media that you choose to draw with as it can really change the mood of the piece.

11

WHAT DO DESIGNERS RESEARCH?   **WHAT IS PRIMARY RESEARCH?**   WHAT IS SECONDARY RESEARCH?

43

12

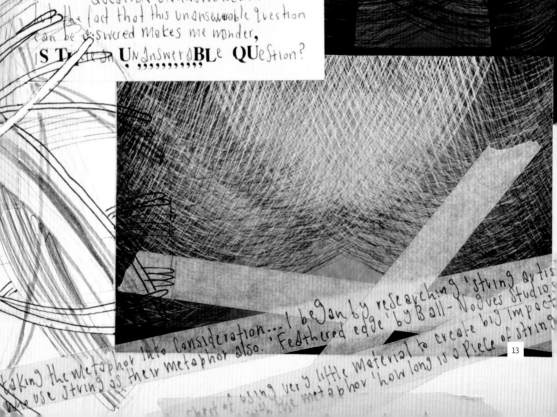

"**H**ow long is a pIeCe of String?"
one of those Questions that almost begs to be
answered... is there **A**n answer?
⊗ to take the Metaphor more **LI**terally, it has
I Cen Made possible to find the approximate
length of **A** PIeCe of string.
TECHNiCALLY.....

A PIeCe of string can **B**e no less than
1/4 of an inch or its **J**ust **A** sample of string
and no more than
100 foot or it **S** technicaly a reel of
string...

apparently a typical Piece Of string is between
one and eight foot... making the average around
3 ft 6 ins... I PERSONALLY DONT THINK THERE IS
ANYTHING WRONG WITH HAVING A
QUESTION UNANSWERED...
the fact that this unanswerable Question
can be answered Makes me wonder,
IS There an UNanswerABLe QUestion?
, " , , , , , , , , , ,

taking the metaphor into consideration... I began by researching ' string artists
who use string as their metaphor also.. 'Feathered edge' by Ball-Nogues studios
... the effect of using very little Material to create big impact...
...with the metaphor 'how long is a Piece of string'

13

Secondary research is information gathered from sources such as books, films, magazines and design work by others. Secondary research is invaluable, especially if you want to see something that is hard to find yourself, for example, seeing snow crystals through a microscope or looking at how arteries branch and flow through the body. It is also critical to help you to understand design concepts such as decoration and ornamentation and to help you to understand the different contexts for textile design. This is called contextual research. However, it is important not to rely solely on secondary research as your visual source of inspiration. You are likely to feel more inspired if you go out and look and experience for yourself, and this will undoubtedly affect the way that you develop your visual ideas.

Museums are a great way of undertaking secondary research – they contain an abundance of cultural artefacts for you to see. It is essential though, that you do not simply copy designs from another source – it is your job as a textile researcher to identify and find raw sources that you can develop into your own design work. It is helpful to look at some of the techniques used by other cultures in pattern, structure and textile composition, but it is all about researching and synthesizing what you are researching, so that you can use it in your own way.

14

13
A student's sketchbook page, showing how a brief has been thought through. The brief asked, 'How long is a piece of string?'. The student had to think about this metaphorically and answer the brief, both visually and through text. This student looked at the work of other designers to help her think through her own project brief.

14
A student project board, showing how scientific information about DNA has been researched, collected and related to pattern structure.

Becky Earley is a printed textiles designer, who creates new textile concepts for sustainability through making and academic research. She makes, writes, teaches, manages, mentors and consults. She has her own label, B.Earley, and works for the University of the Arts, London, as Director of the Textile Futures research Centre. She is also a Reader at Chelsea College of Art and Design. Earley's approach is based on thinking and making in order to explore sustainable design, driving innovation and inspiration and creating change. Her process involves reading, talking, watching, and listening. She is known for her use of new and sustainable printing techniques and uses painting, photography theatre and film as a key source of inspiration.

15

▶ **15**

Becky Earley at work. Earley's designs make use of strong contrast elements and she is well known for her commitment to sustainable textiles. In 1999, in response to the mess and toxic waste that some textile production processes created, Earley developed her 'exhaust printing' process. Like exhaust dyeing, exhaust printing reuses the original dye solution for each piece in the production batch, thus recycling chemicals and minimising waste and water pollution. She has also developed a 'heat photogram' method of printing onto fabric and photography has played a big part in her designs ever since.

▶ **16**

One of Becky Earley's painted shirts. These garments are obtained from textile recycling plants and printed on using sustainable methods. Earley also sometimes alters the shirts to create new silhouettes. Earley is constantly looking for new 'reuse' materials, new base fabrics and new colour combinations.

16

J.R. Campbell is Professor and Director of the Fashion School at Kent State University in Kent, Ohio, USA. He has a background as a designer educator, researching and creating art/design work through the use of digital textile design technologies.

HOW DID YOU GET STARTED?

I completed a Bachelors of Science degree in Environmental Design and a Master of Fine Arts in Textile Arts and Costume Design at the University of California at Davis. Following that, I started exhibiting my textile artwork in juried venues and taught at three different art schools in San Francisco (Academy of Art, FIDM, Art Institute International).
I then took a tenure-track faculty position at Iowa State University, which allowed me the opportunity to begin writing grants, conducting research and generating artwork

with digital textile printing technologies. After I received tenure and was promoted to Associate Professor at Iowa State, I decided to take the leap to Scotland to work at the Glasgow School of Art.

WHAT IS THE ENVIRONMENT LIKE IN YOUR STUDIO?

The studio is full of fabric swatches, attempted prints, and so on. in and amongst computers, there is a wide-format digital textile printer, a 60-inch bed laser cutter, a couple of steamers, 15 head embroidery machines and staff to help support the studio as a digital fashion service provider.

CAN YOU TELL ME ABOUT YOUR DESIGN PROCESS? HOW DO YOU GENERATE IDEAS?

Two themes that continue through my work are my interests in visual

18

story-telling and in finding ways to visually describe and push the use of digital tools in textiles. Although I began more in a tradition of textile design, I now almost always design both textile and product concept as one process. The digital tools allow for the creation of end products that have drastically evolved my textile design approach. I sometimes work from my own photography, sketches or digital illustrations to engineer print designs into garment structures.

WHY DO YOU RESEARCH? WHY IS IT IMPORTANT?

The research I do not only helps me to understand the use of the tools and materials, but also helps me to keep perspective on how these tools and designs can be employed to explore creative business models and practices. Put simply, I am interested in helping to evolve the textile and fashion industries, because I am completely enamoured by the medium.

17

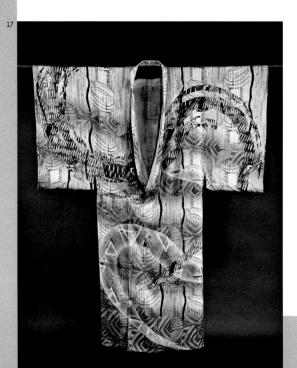

WHAT ARE YOUR MAIN SOURCES OF RESEARCH?

I look to daily news sources, public and trade magazines and scholarly journals to help build my larger arguments about the role of technology in textiles. For my art/design work, I look everywhere – I do a lot of travelling and see everything as a form of texture and motif.

HOW DO YOU START YOUR RESEARCH?

I ask myself what I'd like to say next; my work is generally conceptually driven.

WHAT OR WHO HAS HAD THE MOST INFLUENCE ON YOUR WORK?

I have been strongly influenced by the works of Jack Lenor Larsen, Robert Stewart, Timorous Beasties, Rory Crichton, Junichi Arai, Ana Lisa Hedstrom, Yoshiko Wada, Robert Hillestad, Kerry Mcquire-King, and my great collaborator/colleague Jean Parsons.

WHAT IS YOUR GREATEST ACHIEVEMENT TO DATE?

I don't know! I sometimes get awards for my work that really surprise me. One piece that I feel really was an achievement is a piece that I created for the 'New Craft Future Voices' conference in Dundee (2007). The piece, called 'Wearing this distorted space', comes closest in describing the experience of working digitally with textiles to convey a connection between our environments and build alternative perceptions of our physical spaces.

DO YOU HAVE ANY ADVICE TO THOSE THINKING OF A CAREER IN TEXTILE DESIGN?

Follow your passion and always be thinking about where you would like to be in five years. Make every decision be based in attaining that goal.

17
'Charles Rennie Mackintosh: Fingerprint Kimono'. Digitally printed silk satin and twill: reversible kimono.

18
'Mackintosh Re-Interpreted Chrysanthemum Repeat'. Digitally printed cotton velvet.

19
'Transformation: Icarus II'. Digitally printed silk habotai garment. Collaboration with Jean Parsons.

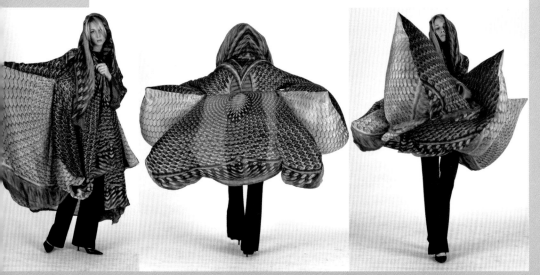

DO NOT LEAVE
SPOONS IN
PIGMENT TUBS
wash and put away after use

DO NOT LEAVE
SPOONS IN
PIGMENT TUBS

SCARLE   (CUSTARD)   (LEMON)   GREEN
YELLOW   YELLOW

1

3

THE TOOLKIT

This chapter will discuss what you should consider in order to undertake research for textile design. It will look at the physical and metaphorical toolkit for both primary and secondary research, enabling a deeper understanding of different approaches to research. Research should always underpin a designer's process as this helps to ensure that design development into a product is current, relevant, innovative and exciting. Research is the fundamental basis of any design produced for the marketplace. Research also plays a critical role in the creative wellbeing of the designer themself as it allows them to expand their own knowledge, find out new things and open up new horizons. Research for textiles should include materials and visualization processes at every stage of production, and it is vital that there is a holistic design approach between context, materials and visuals throughout.

1
The list of tools available to the textile designer is endless. What you use and how you use it will be entirely up to you.

Primary research is a vital part of a student's search for information as it involves seeking details that will be of use in developing textile designs. It is important to understand primary research in two ways. Firstly, there is primary visual research, which requires you to see or notice things that are of interest to you. For example, old paint cracking and peeling from a wall may be rich in colour, surface texture and pattern, or observing intricate scaffolding and building work in progress may give you interesting structures and forms. Primary visual research can be anything that you feel has the potential to lend itself to the development of textiles. There is certainly a wealth of visual information out there – the secret ingredient is you. You must feel excited by what you are seeing and be tuned in to elements in the environment which contain rich visual information about textures, forms, patterns, structures and colour. Try to analyze what you are seeing at all times, even when you are not drawing, as this is a skill that needs practice. As you become more experienced, you will soon find yourself doing it everywhere!

Secondly, there is primary contextual research, which requires you to look, think and explore the world of textiles through experiencing textiles themselves. This will include handling cloth, using cloth, observing people and cloth and so on. This way, you will build up knowledge and an understanding regarding cloth; how it acts, drapes, moves and how people use and live with it. Remember that you are designing for people and you must think about this as a designer.

2
Looking, finding and recording interesting patterns in the environment counts as primary research. These bottle tops show great pattern, texture and colour – three key ingredients that a textile designer can develop further into designs.

3
A student observation sheet, showing how to examine a primary source. This student has considered colour, pattern, contours and forms using inks and wash. Sheets like this can be a good starting point in the development of design work.

2

3

THE SKETCHBOOK

The sketchbook is the most important tool that you have! They come in many different shapes and sizes from small A5 (5.8" × 8.3") to larger A2 (C). They can be bound hardbacks, spiral–bound or loosely bound at the top to enable pages to be taken out. You should decide which is the best size to use depending on how you intend to use it. For example, do you want to carry it with you at all times to record your thoughts as well as your observations? If so, an A2 (C) might be too large. Do you want the pages to come out? If so, the bound hardbacks will not be suitable. Before you buy, think about how you will use it and buy one to suit you and the way that you work.

Think of the sketchbook as your creative companion. Record primary visual information through drawing and write your ideas and observations down. Include information on artists and designers that you feel inspired by. This can be postcards from exhibitions, information on colour and contextual resources. The sketchbook is a reflective tool that allows you to go back and forward through your research and development in a continuous way.

DRAWING MATERIALS

Before you start to draw, it is vital that you choose materials to draw with that empathize with the source. Essentially, this means that you must think about the source and materials as one, and choose materials that will best translate this. It is helpful to think about your source in the following way: is the source fragile, solid, transparent, opaque, rich and colourful? Then choose materials that will contribute to the feel or mood of the object that you are drawing. For example, imagine that you are looking at a shiny, silver, structural and angular object that has a sharp, clean and highly tonal reflective profile. What would you use to draw it? Paint? Charcoal? Pencil? Ink? Collage? You must think about the qualities of the object – is it solid, reflective, sharp? Relate these to a medium that will best render these qualities. Soft charcoal may be too light and wispy to capture the stark tones, sharp edges and weighty solidity; however, hard black charcoal would capture it well. Take time to think about what you are looking at and always analyze the qualities of the object that you are drawing in order to select an appropriate medium to draw with.

4
Choosing the appropriate drawing materials from your toolkit needs careful thought, as the medium should empathize with the source. You need to take time and think about the best way to translate your source. Don't always choose the medium that you feel most comfortable with – try to be experimental with your initial research drawings.

4

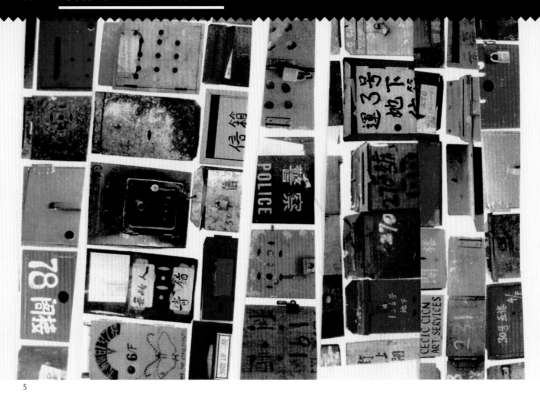

5

PHOTOGRAPHY

Photography is an excellent way to gather primary information but you must think about how you use your camera to gather it. The camera is your research tool and not a quick snapping device! Remember that you are searching and recording imagery through the camera to develop further. Think carefully about what you compose in the frame. Make decisions about composition and how light and colour are balanced. Are you close enough to see the textures or surfaces that you need for your research? Have you captured and composed the structures that will be of use to you? The camera provides a different type of visual research; it has its own qualities that can be exploited fully in the development process. Try not to think of photographs as simply 'prints to draw from', as you are far better making the drawing on site if possible. Instead, think of photographs and photography as a different medium that has its own unique qualities to explore.

Like your sketchbook, try and choose a camera to suit your needs. Are you going to carry your camera with you at all times? Do you need a fairly compact one? You may need to find one that will allow you to get good close-ups.

'A photograph is not only an image (as a painting is an image), an interpretation of the real; it is also a trace, something directly stencilled off the real, like a footprint or a death mask.'
SUSAN SONTAG

CAD

Computers are a fantastic way to play and experiment with visual imagery, and programs like Adobe Photoshop and Illustrator allow you to further develop initial ideas that you have recorded through drawing or photography. It is crucial, however, that your visual research does not begin with the computer. Avoid drawing things directly on the computer when you do not have any of your own visual research, otherwise you risk making stereotypical forms and marks that are without any proper observational skill. Instead, use the computer to play and explore what you can do with your already observed marks and textures, and scan your photographs into the computer and play around with them.

It might be useful to photograph your drawings and then drop them into Photoshop to manipulate them further. It is possible to cut and paste, change colours, and create layer masks of the drawing. The ideas generated from this process can then help to develop the visual research further in the sketchbook. In this way, the computer is a means to develop ideas, and not just a tool for producing final design work (which is what it is normally used for in many areas of design, including digital textile design).

'Even when I work with computers, with high technology, I always try to put in the touch of the hand.'
ISSEY MIYAKE

5
Using photographs to cut, collage and manipulate is a great way to develop design ideas. Make sure that you only use your own photography if you decide to work this way, as using other people's work has copyright issues.

6
Computers can be used to further develop visual research and also to explore secondary research areas.

7
A student moodboard showing
how secondary visual research can
help to describe the colours, textures
and feel for the direction
of your work.

8
Looking at what others are doing
will help you to understand how
textiles are being used.

LOUR

r is a dominating influenc

t pastels in Modern

ds of Pool Party

– on its own

– n ted

dy

ds arm

s – touches of m

BRICS

– set to continue as a fabric reflecting

up shine of the season

arents – fabrics with see-through qualities such as fine laces

8

Secondary research is different from primary research in that you do not experience a phenomenon yourself, but instead see it through the eyes of someone else. This applies to both visual and contextual research. Secondary research is crucial to help deepen and expand your knowledge of textiles and textile design. You can use books, the Internet, TV documentaries or films to find out more about any subject.

Secondary research enables you to find out about new materials and to discover what other new developments are happening within the textiles arena. Through secondary research, you discover things about your subject on a global scale and this helps to build your own knowledge base. Therefore, secondary research is just as important as primary research and you must be able to balance both.

PERIODICALS

Periodicals refer to scholarly publications that are produced at regular intervals. Within textile design, this would normally be a journal, which contains a collection of written pieces that are up to date and current. Publications such as *Textile – The Journal of Cloth and Culture*, which contains articles that are fairly brief and authoritative in that they have been written and reviewed by experts in their field, is an example of a textiles periodical.

These publications will give you varied types of information regarding a whole range of issues relating to textiles. This might include gender debates and the politics of work, historical debates, craft methods or current research practices. They are important publications that inform the audience about current debates and practices within the wider area of textiles. Crucially they are a key means by which information based on scholarly research is shared throughout the field. College and university libraries normally house journals that relate to the subjects being taught.

MAGAZINES

Magazines are an excellent way to access popular topics that relate to your subject area and there is an abundance of them to choose from. They vary in the type of information they contain and many of them focus on fashion or interior textile products. Some specialist textile publications like *Selvedge*, *Textile ETN Forum* and *Embroidery Magazine*, devote the entire publication to textiles and textile issues. Fashion forecasting magazines like *Textile View* are essential for textile students as they contain information regarding forecasting trends that are used within the textiles industry to develop colour palettes, yarns, fabrics and patterns for the marketplace.

There are also fantastic technology magazines full of all the latest information on new materials and fabrics. Magazines such as *Materials KTN*, *Smart Textiles* and *Nano Technology and Future Materials* centre on textile innovations such as spider silk, ceramic yarn and conductive inks. Such information can help you to understand the breadth of the area that you are working within and becomes quite important as you become more experienced.

Popular magazines such as *Elle Decoration*, *World of Interiors* and *Vogue* also feature textiles frequently. Essentially, they have visual information (photography) of fashion and interior design, and feature articles regarding various popular topics. It is worth browsing more mainstream fashion and interiors magazines, as they are excellent snapshots of contemporary popular culture.

'Research is first –
if you're not interested, you
never can find something.'
ISSEY MIYAKE

9
Periodicals can help you to keep up to date with your subject area. Try to read these publications as often as you can as they will help to contextualize your work. Buying them can be costly, but college libraries often keep them in their collections.

9

AUTHOR TIP	10	i–D	Textile View
The following publications are of particular interest to textile designers:	Another Magazine	Issue One	View on Colour
	Bloom	Lula	Viewpoint
	Blueprint	Marie Claire	Vogue
	Dazed & Confused	Marmalade	
	Elle	Nylon	
	Elle Decoration	Selvedge	
	Fibrearts	Tank	
	Frieze	Textile Forum	

10

BOOKS

Books are a great source of inspiration. Within textile design, there is a vast wealth of books available. Textbooks are particularly beneficial to people who are learning a new process, as they help to direct practical knowledge. But there are also books available to help build your knowledge in many areas of textile design. They include books about well-known designers, design movements such as Bauhaus, theoretical books, historical textiles and cultures and so on. The list is enormous! Essentially, books help you to further your own practice and help you to think about and analyze subjects. This ultimately helps you to understand textile design within many different contexts.

PLACES TO VISIT

Getting out and about is a very important part of being a designer. It is necessary for primary research collection, but is also crucial to help you find out what others are doing first hand. It's good to visit places where people make or sell textiles. Shops like Liberty's in London are a joy to visit for any textile designer as they house design products that range from clothing to blankets. Keep an eye on what's out there via the Internet as designers' websites contain many products and prices for you to see. It is also a good idea to visit places where people make and sell their own work, such as artists' studios, craft fairs and open days where you can talk to practitioners themselves.

11

12

GALLERIES AND MUSEUMS

Galleries and museums are a genuine source of inspiration that make you think about and reflect on your own work. Museums are an excellent source of visual inspiration and they provide us with knowledge about the history of a culture as well as the products of cultures and nature. The good news is that there are museums in almost every city in the world!

Galleries tend to focus on contemporary artefacts and practices, although many have a permanent collection that exemplifies art and design from an historical perspective. Galleries vary what they show and many focus on fine art, which includes paintings, sculptures, conceptual pieces, films, videos, photography and installations. Some galleries focus on design, such as the Design Museum in London, or the Cooper Hewitt National Design Museum in New York, and others show contemporary craft. Look up galleries in your area and find some that show contemporary

products for you to visit. Going to see current exhibitions is a great way of keeping up to date with what is going on and meeting people!

10
Street market stalls such as the one shown here can provide photographic information on pattern, repeat, colour and form.

11
Places of cultural heritage, such as the architecture and interior design of opulent palaces, stately homes and places of religious interest, can be easily sourced and are full of rich decorative detail for textile research.

12
The Sagrada Familia in Barcelona, Spain. This monumental, unfinished cathedral by Antoni Gaudi is heavily influenced by forms of nature.

Based in Seattle, USA, Maggie Orth describes herself as an 'artist and technologist who invents interactive textiles'. She is one of the first creative and technical practitioners of electronic textiles; 'textiles that integrate conductive elements, often yarns or fibres into the textile'. Orth's work focuses on colour-change textiles and touch-sensitive light textiles. She has been exhibited widely across the USA, Europe and Japan.

▶ 13
PILE BLOCKS

'Pile Blocks is an interactive textile touch sensor and light artwork that continues Maggie's investigation of the perceptual properties of electronic textiles. By touching the woven pile squares (the grey conductive areas), light is transmitted through the woven textile to reveal hidden colour and pattern. Touching the different pile sensors creates different animated lighting patterns, which move over the surface of the piece. Patterns interact with each other like ripples in a pond.

A single piece of fabric combining both double-weave and pile textile structures creates the conductive sensors and light-transmitting effects. When white, LED light passes through the double weave fabric and the coloured weaving on the back is revealed. Software explores a variety of regular patterns and randomly generated sequences.'

Media: Conductive yarn, cotton yarn, LEDs, custom-drive electronics and expressive software. 56.5" × 27" × 2.5" (143.51cm × 68.58cm × 6.35cm).

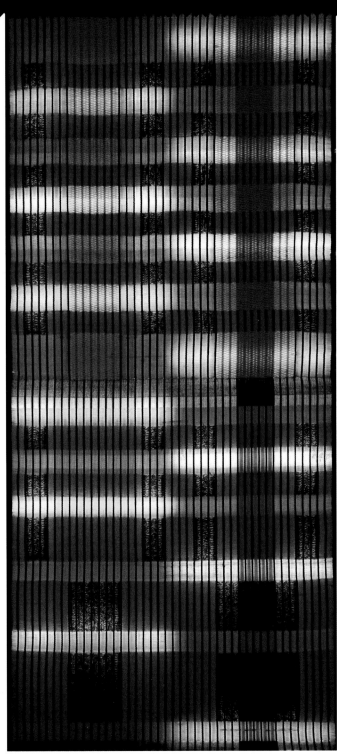

13

Linda Florence designs and handprints wallpaper. She trained in textiles but now works in print and illustration. She designs her wallpapers and prints them to order for clients. Printing her own papers allows her to personalize each project and change colours to the customer's request. This also allows her to make the designs change across a room, working with the architecture. Linda also designs specifically for one-off projects. She has designed wallpapers for Ted Baker's shops worldwide. On some of the projects, she has printed the wallpapers and on others designed the patterns, which are then laser-cut for use inside and outside the stores.

WHERE DO YOU WORK?

I work at home and in my studio. In my studio I enjoy being surrounded by my paints, fabrics and sketchbooks but I also have work at home as living with my wallpapers lets me see them change in different lights during the day. The foils which embellish some of my wallpapers catch the light and change from morning to evening.

WHAT INSPIRES YOU?

Everything and anything; my work is a collage of pattern and shape from around my life. I have always been attracted to patterns. I love gathering scraps and finding new textures and materials. My imagery includes traditional William Morris. I love drawing in the V&A archives, maze patterns, Bridget Riley paintings and also imagery from my childhood like Space Invaders and Pac Men.

WHAT OR WHO HAS HAD THE MOST INFLUENCE ON YOUR WORK?

Artists and designers inspire me. They include Jim Lambie, Brigit Riley, Do-Ho-Suh, Robert Orchardson, Macintosh, Morris, Timorous Beasties, Concrete Blond, Zaha Hadid, Giles Deacon, Basso and Brook.

HOW DO YOU LIKE TO WORK?

I love to experiment. My work is always trying things out. I never do standard print or textiles. I print with varnish or floor paint or work with fabric and paper but also concrete or slate or wood or sugar! I really love to have freedom to try new materials and develop patterns and layouts.

I try to mix different scales together with large Space Invaders layers with Morris-inspired damask patterns and small maps. I also mix unusual colours together. My colour palette is constantly changing and developing with my work. I love working with clients to perhaps change a colour to be especially for them, making it unique to them and their homes.

14
Linda Florence uses both handprinting and other technologies to realize her design work.

15
An example of Linda Florence's designs for floors.

'A designer is a planner
with an aesthetic sense'.
BRUNO MUNARI

1

4

PLANNING RESEARCH

In previous chapters, we have discussed what research for textiles involves and the tools needed to carry out both primary and secondary research. In this chapter, we explore the planning stage before work begins on your research project. A project requires planning, particularly in the initial stages. With careful thought on how you intend to approach your project, you will have made sure that you have considered all areas for potential research. Planning also provides you with a safety net, a foundation of ideas which you can refer back to during any stage of your textile project.

1
Planning your research is crucial. Thinking ahead about what papers or materials to use, where to go to find information and what tools to take with you, should be thought through before you embark on your research.

How you start a project will depend to a large extent on the type of brief set. Some projects have an open framework, perhaps based around a theme, word or concept, in which you can make personal decisions on how and where to research. Other types of briefs can be more specific requiring a focused approach from the beginning in order to develop a body of work for a particular type of outcome.

SET BRIEF

A set brief will usually provide you with a number of parameters or guidelines which you must consider throughout the design process. These can include working with a particular type of media, colour palette or context. Textile briefs for fashion will often ask that you respond to a particular trend, colour palette and context. Alternatively, you may be asked to design textiles for an interior context, for example a large public space, where the design work must respond to the function and usage of the building.

LIVE PROJECTS

Often projects in this category are in direct collaboration with an industrial partner or design company. Known as 'live' projects, they provide an opportunity to work on commercially relevant themes where communication, site visits and feedback with the company are often possible throughout key stages.

THEME

Words and images may be used as the creative catalyst for starting your research project. The advantage of this approach is the manner in which you can personalize the project by providing a unique creative perspective. They can be used to express your own individuality, your viewpoints and interests. It is important to remember that good designers bring their own narrative to design, which is vital for creating your own visual language.

2
This presentation board shows how this student is exploring landscapes for a fashion knitwear brief. There is a clear connection between the photography at the centre of the board and the textures and colours in the knitted samples.

2

3

When considering a theme, you need to select a starting point that will stimulate you creatively. As we mentioned previously, this will need to be considered in relation to the brief. Often, themes can be developed from a word or an image. As a catalyst, they can then be used as a creative springboard for brainstorming, which is covered on pages 74–75.

There are a number of different approaches for generating a theme that we will now explore.

ABSTRACT

This is where a random word or situation is used as inspiration. Often referred to as a surrealist approach, this method stimulates a range of ideas by using metaphors (a way of understanding one thing or idea in relation to another). The words are then developed into a number of visual research ideas.

NARRATIVE

This is where an account of something is used to explore design ideas. This could be a story or poem, which can then be used to conjure up visual references and imagery. Freddie Robins is well known for her playful, witty and subversive knitted textiles. She uses the soft materials of knitting to tell stories, which in other mediums may otherwise seem macabre. In her piece 'Knitted Homes of

'Every season I find myself working with new themes, sometimes even ones that oppose each other. For example, Clements Riberio once asked for over-the-top designs for a collection they described as "Frida Kahlo meets Singapore whorehouse", while John Rocha wanted minimal designs that evoked abstract art.'
KAREN NICOL

4

Crime', tea cosies are knitted to represent the British homes of women who have killed, or the houses in which they have killed. 'I've always been obsessed with murder and what makes people feel they could kill, when for most of us that sort of behavior is so outside the moral code', she explains.

CONCEPTUAL

In this approach, a number of references are brought together to develop an idea. Emphasis is placed on investigating ideas through problem solving. Often referred to as lateral thinking or thinking outside of the box, conceptual projects encourage an open mind, free to explore ideas from new perspectives. Lucy Orta's work centres around humanitarian design. In her work *Refuge Wear* she places emphasis on the plight of the homeless by developing experimental textiles that explore the relationship between clothing and architecture.

3
Freddie Robins' *Knitted Homes of Crime* uses the non-threatening tea cosie as a metaphor for exploring controversial issues within society.

4
Lucy Orta's *Refuge Wear* examines textiles and clothing within the urban environment. Her work addresses concerns regarding displaced communities.

system for
analising
language

Literal language
refers to words
that do not
deviate from their
defined meaning

Figurative
language refers to
words, and groups
of words, that
exaggerate or alter
the usual meanings
of the component
words.

Rhetoric is the
art of using
language to
communicate
effectively

literal

figurative

rhetoric

language

how long is
a piece of
string

metaphor

analogy
between
two objects
or ideas

Metaphor
also denotes
rhetorical
figures of
speech that
achieve their
effects via
association,
comparison,
or
resemblance

simile

comparison

Simile is
a comparison
between two
different things that
resemble each other
in at least one way –
often introduced
with the words
'like', 'as' or 'than'

In formal prose the
simile is a device both
of art and explanation,
comparing an
unfamiliar thing to
some familiar thing

5

At the beginning of a project, it is important to be open-minded and receptive to new ideas and different ways of thinking. At this early stage, you will want to explore a broad range of ideas and thoughts around a particular theme, brief or even a single word. This is an exciting phase where you can really think outside of the box, so stretch the boundaries of the brief by considering every possible idea around the given theme.

BRAINSTORMING AND MIND MAPPING TECHNIQUES

The term 'brainstorming' is commonly used to describe methods for generating initial ideas quickly. Group sessions are very helpful in this situation but brainstorming can also be effective when done on your own. In group situations, ideas and thoughts can be shared to help broaden areas of thinking. Usually, one person from the group will be responsible for writing down all the words. A word or an image is enough, rather than a long description. When all possible thoughts have been investigated, the list of words is often extensive. Now you can begin to re-examine this list again. Decide on the words that are the most important. Highlight key words and towards the end of the brainstorming session put these into a list of priority. The work generated from this session can now be used as a reference point both at the start of and throughout the life of your project.

The method described above is one way in which to generate ideas. Another method commonly used for brainstorming is mind mapping. Mind maps are visual maps of ideas. Starting with a central idea they span out from this, usually in a circular shape. As you draw branches from your central idea, you add on key words, colours and images. They are an excellent tool as they can help you to visualize your thinking, by breaking down your thoughts into the most important key words – making it easier to make connections and associations.

'It is better to have enough ideas for some of them to be wrong, than to be always right by having no ideas at all.'
EDWARD DE BONO

5
A student mind map, showing how a brief has been approached. The brief in this instance is open as it asks students themselves to find an area to research, using 'metaphor' as the research method.

KNITTED JEWELLERY

THE KNIT WEARS
THE PERSON OR
THE PERSON
WEARS THE KNIT?

6

'Inspiration is usually very indirect; it can take lots of different shapes and forms which can also be influenced by timing. To name but a few: Dutch design, Josef Frank, William Morris, Joseph Beuys, Paul Klee, Leonardo, Picasso, Ridley Scott, Tom Kirk, Chuck Mitchell, Italian Motorcycles, Jake and Dinos Chapman, Ricky Gervais, Mona Hatoum and so on.'

TIMOROUS BEASTIES

6
A student board, showing a playful approach to knit. Being playful can help to direct your work in ways that you may not have considered before.

FINDING THE INFORMATION YOU NEED TO START THE PROJECT

In the previous section, we discussed brainstorming techniques and how these might be used at the beginning of a project. Now we will focus on how to use this information.

Brainstorming will have helped you to start thinking about your project and should have sparked off a number of possibilities. It will now help to make a list of places where you'll find information to further expand your research. This should include both primary and secondary source material, as discussed in previous chapters.

To start with, we will discuss finding information from primary research sources. The best place to start is with you. What information is directly available to you within your own environment, your everyday life and in your cultural and personal background? We all have different points of visual reference – whether these come from our travels, our homes, our pasttimes or the places we like to visit. All of these day-to-day experiences contain rich sources of visual information, which we can put to good use. Consider firstly how these might be appropriate for your project.

The next area to consider is your access to wider sources of primary research. Do you know how you might gain access to certain sites of information? Public buildings, for example museums, galleries and railway stations are all easily accessible and contain both primary and secondary sources. Who do you know that can perhaps provide you with additional access and information? Consider contacting organizations or companies that might be of interest and able to help you out with your research.

TRENDFORECASTING

Trendforecasting, also known as trend analysis, is concerned with predicting future changes in society. Operating as a zeitgeist for textiles and fashion, this usually encompasses colour forecasting, trends occurring in pattern, and changes in materials and in the form of garments and accessories. Many businesses within the textile industry rely on forecasting information to inform the design direction of their fashion and fabric collections. As a textile designer, an understanding of trends is required, particularly when designing for commercial markets. Depending on the type of project brief, trend sources are often used as a starting point where a number of forecasting websites and periodicals are available.

MIND-MAPPING EXERCISE

Starting in the middle of a blank page, write down or draw the idea that you intend to develop. For this we suggest that you use the page in landscape orientation.

Begin to develop related sub-headings around this central theme, connecting each of them to the centre with a line.

Using the same process for the sub-headings, generate another layer of lower-level sub-headings connecting each of those to the corresponding sub-theme.

'I trawl flea markets, car boot sales and vintage boutiques for amazing items. That's where I look for vintage textiles, old embroideries and pieces of haberdashery, as well as things that have incredible colours, fantastic textures and interesting histories. I decorate the studio with it all, and it transforms my studio into one big moodboard.'

KAREN NICOL

CONTEXTUAL RESEARCH

Contextual research is research that investigates who you are designing for. An understanding of the context or the type of person that you are designing for is paramount to ensure that your design work is highly relevant. Often this information can be set within the brief, or you might be asked to identify a particular context yourself. This requires researching both through secondary source information such as contemporary magazines and periodicals, and also carrying out primary research by visiting retail outlets and designer shops and talking to and observing potential user groups.

HISTORICAL ARCHIVES

As a textile designer, it is important that you develop a good understanding of the rich heritage of textiles. By researching previous textile designs from over the centuries, we are able to understand how and why certain fabrics were created and to question their relevance to design today and for the future. Design companies such as Timorous Beasties are well-known for referencing past collections through new contemporary representations. In particular their play on traditional Toile de Jouy fabrics (historical fabrics that depicted day-to-day scenes) such as Glasgow Toile and London Toile depicts contemporary scenes within a historical pattern (see page 22).

For textiles, historical research can come from many different sources, some directly related to textiles, for example through fashion, interiors and furnishing, and through other design subjects such as ceramics, jewellery and costume. Large galleries and museums are often wonderful places to find a vast selection of decorative arts in one place. But there are also many smaller collections available in other national and regional galleries and museums. Often, appointments can be made with the collection's curator to view certain periods or types of artefacts from the museum or gallery archive, which are not on public display.

7
A student moodboard, using old photographs and imagery from the past. These have been used to encapsulate the theme, which was 'the nostalgic romance of war'.

USING THE LIBRARY

The library is often the best place to start exploring a research project as you have instant access to a wide range of reference material, both text and image-based. After brainstorming you will have some idea about where to start looking. When visiting the library, try to be open minded and allow plenty of time to explore different sections and book aisles on subjects that might at first seem unrelated to your project. Unlike the Internet, using a book is a completely different type of experience, being both visually stimulating and physically inspiring through the physical touch and smell that is offers. It is important to remember that books in themselves are beautifully crafted objects. Looking at the layout of contemporary and original, historical manuscripts can provide far more enriching sources of inspiration than are likely to be found on any website page.

8
There are thousands of great books about textile design on the market, and most of them showcase a range of inspirational work. College or public libraries are a good place to start your search. When you find a book that you like, look up the bibliography at the back – this can provide you with an invaluable list for further investigation.

9
Libraries are an excellent source of inspiration. Try to look at books covering other creative disciplines, such as fine art and graphic design, as well as those covering textiles.

USING THE INTERNET

The Internet is by far the most accessible method for finding and gathering information today. Through the use of search engines, we can immediately find an enormous number of linked websites and sources for researching any subject worldwide. The Internet is a vital tool for finding information quickly and providing us with up-to-date design trends and commentary. It is, however, important not to rely solely on Internet research for projects. It is fantastic for putting us in touch with companies and specialist information. However, Internet research should never be used alons. Other types of research need to be used in conjunction with these methods to keep us in touch with other considerations; the tactile quality of materials and three-dimensional forms and patterns, for example.

10
Internet research is one of the quickest and easiest methods available to the textile designer. It should, however, always be used in conjunction with other methods.

10

EXPLORING THE THEME EXERCISE

Select an event that you've experienced over the past year. Consider how you might research this using your own touch, taste, sight, smell and hearing.

How might you research this using secondary sources? Where could you visit? Which books could you look at?

How might you research this using the Internet? What sort of sites do you think might be most helpful?

at Paco Rabanne. His designs are known for their use of both vivid colours and unusual effects (such as computer technology and flashing lights) and more traditional Indian crafts such as embroidery, appliqué and beading. Since launching his own label in 2007, his creations have earned him worldwide recognition and a large fan-base.

Arora's collection for autumn/winter 2011 showcases his own theatrical and exuberant style. Inspired by the magic dolls of the German artist, Annie Hoffstater, he uses brightly coloured textures together with lace open cutwork to create an eclectic and exciting collection of textile surfaces.

Johanna Basford is a freelance illustrator and surface pattern designer. Companies or design studios commission her to create artwork for them. They set a brief outlining the specifications of what they need; she then hand-draws the artwork before scanning into Photoshop for final tweaks and adjustments, and then provides the artwork to them as high-resolution digital files. Her clients then transfer this artwork to its final application, be that a website, packaging, products or editorial print.

HOW DID YOU GET STARTED?

Initially, when I left art school in 2005, I worked as a designer/maker. I designed and made my own collections of interiors products, such as wallpapers, fabrics, cushions, lighting and ceramics. All my products were either made by myself in my screen printing studio or manufactured in small batches. I then sold these products either directly to consumers or wholesale to retailers and agents.

I worked exclusively in black and white, hand-drawing all my designs with minimal use of CAD. The emphasis of my design work was on highly detailed, intricate visuals. I began to receive commissions to create artwork for other brands and companies – clients who liked my style of work and wanted to apply it to their own products or projects.

As my business developed, it became clear that my passion lay in the creation of the artwork, not in manufacturing products. In late 2009, I decided to cease making my own range of products and focus solely on freelance commission work.

13

13
Johanna's studio shows how designers pin up ideas that they are working on in order to have it 'out in the open'. This is so that they can look and think about it even if they are working on something else.

WHERE DO YOU WORK?

I work with clients all over the world in cities such as London, Paris, New York, Stockholm and San Francisco. I work from a small studio at home, where I have my drawing desk and computer equipment. I travel to meet clients in Edinburgh, Glasgow and London about once a month, although a lot of my client contact is via email, phone and Skype.

WHAT IS THE ENVIRONMENT LIKE IN YOUR STUDIO?

I like to work in an organized environment. Productivity and time management is very important. It's essential that tasks such as admin, book-keeping and client contacts are handled efficiently, other wise they take vast amounts of time and prevent me from concentrating on design work. My studio has lots of storage space for documents, files and drawings, a large desk and a big wall which I use for planning and creating ever-evolving moodboards of inspiration.

CAN YOU TELL ME ABOUT YOUR DESIGN PROCESS? HOW DO YOU GENERATE IDEAS?

Normally I'm working from a client brief. Sometimes these are very specific, other times they are more open and the client leaves it to me to come up with the ideas. I always sketch out initial ideas; layouts, rough shapes, etc. I make lists of the content to be included in the design, then use the Internet or library to find visual references for things I am unfamiliar with.

I then begin creating the design. I work on large, loose sheets of layout paper, initially in pencil then in ink. I scan the final pen-and-ink drawing into Photoshop in very high resolution (up to 1200dpi) and do any final amendments and tweaks, then supply the artwork to the client as a digital file. The hand-drawn artwork is always much larger than the final print size, as this allows me to scale down the artwork in Photoshop.

Some clients request the creation of three rough drafts, which they then review and feedback on. The client then selects which option they would like to develop (or sometimes areas from several different options) and I then return to the artwork and create a final version.

WHY DO YOU RESEARCH? WHY IS IT IMPORTANT?

Every image I create is drawn by hand in pen and ink. In order for me to draw something, I usually require a visual reference. Research for me takes the form of creating large libraries of image files and bookmarks on the web, or finding image references in books and magazines.

I consciously research images for a specific project, but I'm always on the lookout for interesting images and visual references which I store for later use. I do not keep sketchbooks.

WHAT ARE YOUR MAIN SOURCES OF RESEARCH?

I use the Internet a lot. Books and magazines are good, but often a lot of designers are looking at the same resources and you risk creating work which is similar to one of your contemporaries.

Working from real-life sources, such as botanical life, is always a pleasure but in reality, this is very rarely possible. The time and resources required to source and store items is vast – and commercially, you need to work as quickly and efficiently as possible.

HOW DO YOU START YOUR RESEARCH?

I read the brief, speak to the client, then create lists of references that I need to find. I create folders on the computer for each project, then find image references for each item on the list and save them to the folder.

WHAT OR WHO HAS HAD THE MOST INFLUENCE ON YOUR WORK?

My clients, consumers and my contemporaries. When a client sets a brief they generally know what they are after. It's my job to realize that brief and bring their ideas to life. I always try to interpret the brief for them in a way which I feel is creative and unique, but there are always certain elements which have to be done a certain way, be that due to brand identity, printing processes or print budgets.

Consumers (not trend forecasters) decide whether design is successful or not. Ultimately, we need to satisfy the tastes of the consumers who will buy or use the end-product, so it's important to both me and my client to create a design that appeals to the target market.

The work of other creatives, be they my contemporaries or artists and designers throughout history, will always have a certain degree of influence on my work. I was told in art school to 'steal not borrow' and I think this is a great rule to work by. Being affected consciously or subconsciously by the work of others is inevitable, but the important thing is to take the elements of others' work that spark your imagination and develop them into your own practice. You have to make everything your own, not just lift off the page of another designer's portfolio.

15

WHAT IS YOUR GREATEST ACHIEVEMENT TO DATE?

Being commissioned to illustrate the cover of the 2010 Edinburgh Festival Fringe programme was pretty cool. Winning awards is always nice! I also got an Elle Decoration Design Award in 2007 and a Channel 4 Talent Award in 2009.

14

DO YOU HAVE ANY ADVICE FOR THOSE THINKING OF A CAREER IN TEXTILE DESIGN?

Be open-minded and flexible. Don't try and pigeon hole yourself into one discipline or industry sector, but be open to working on as many varied projects with as many differently skilled people as possible. I think you learn so much from collaborating and working in areas out of your preconceived comfort zone.

I'd also advise trying to find some way of making yourself and your work different from the crowd. Business people use the term 'Unique Selling Point' (USP) for this. I think differentiating yourself from the masses and making your work stand out helps make you memorable, raises your profile and most importantly puts you in a niche category, which is always going to be smaller and make it easier to rise to the top.

For example, I work predominately – although not exclusively – in black and white. My signature style of work is very delicate, hand-penned illustrations. Working in this style has helped both to build my profile as a designer and to single me and my work out from the thousands of other designers and illustrators.

16

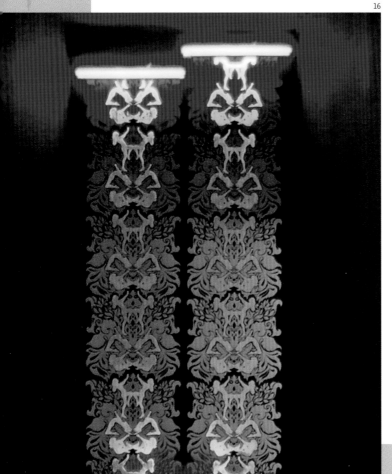

14
Johanna Basford's design work for Converse trainers. Being a surface designer means that Johanna can apply her designs to a number of different 'surfaces'.

15
Johanna Basford's design work transfers across textiles to include design for illustration.

16
Johanna Basford's commissioned glow wallpaper, which she designed and printed using special ultraviolet-sensitive inks.

'You can find inspiration in everything; if you can't find it then you're not looking properly.'
PAUL SMITH

1

5

OBSERVATION AND ANALYSIS

This chapter takes an in-depth look at the techniques used for observation and analysis in textile design. We have divided these into five key areas: colour, surface, structure, texture and pattern.

Inspiration can come from anywhere; from the natural world, the urban landscape and your own surroundings, and from sources that you personally find visually exciting and interesting. How you look, observe, record and analyze this information is vitally important, as this visual research is the foundation on which your design work rests.

This chapter describes in detail how to extract visual information from these key themes, from a wide variety of sources.

1
Aerial view of patterned landscape illustrating natural pattern and colour within the rural environment.

2

2
Sources of colour can be found
all around us. The material
surface and reflection of light will
have an impact on the quality
of colour. From a simple image
of balloons, we can see how
light and shade create numerous
colours and shades.

Colour for textiles can come from a number of different starting points. Primarily, our colour palette will originate from our own visual sources. As we observe and analyze these, we need to find the right methods for capturing a particular type of colour, contrast, tone and proportion. Often, designers are provided with a particular colour palette to reflect a client's colour story or season. Working on interior projects, the use of colour might be pre-determined by the architect or by an existing colour scheme. The context for your textile collection will be a major factor in how you work with colour.

'I am attracted by pure colours. Colours from my childhood, from the Ukraine. Memories of peasant weddings in my country, in which the red and green dresses decorated with many ribbons billowed in dance. Memories of an album of folk costumes brought from Sweden by my uncle.'
SONIA DELAUNAY

COLOUR AND CULTURE

In order to understand the importance of colour, we first of all need to consider its significance within global cultures.

Interpretations of colour differ widely from culture to culture, reflecting both the contemporary and historical aspects of individual societies. In the West, for example, black is often linked with death, but in the East, it is white that carries this meaning.

In the past, many societies have also restricted the use of colour to certain members and classes of society. The number of colours worn by a person could, for example, determine a person's position in society. Today, we still see the remains of these colour restrictions and codes in dress, through school uniforms, the armed services, sports team colours, academic hoods and gowns, and religious wear.

Therefore, we can see that, as humans, we have very strong cultural and emotional relationships with colour. Its physical presence at any particular point in history can create either visual harmony or disruption.

THE LANGUAGE OF COLOUR

Some common colour connotations (mainly found in Western cultures) are listed below.

RED   Red symbolizes passion, fire, blood and desire and is associated with energy, war, danger, strength and power. It is widely used for declaring love or rage. It has very high visibility, which is why stop signs, stop lights and fire equipment are usually painted red. Red lights mean stop but 'come on' in a red light district. In Eastern cultures, red symbolizes happiness.

BLUE   Blues are even more contradictory. Blue is for sunny sky and calm sea, serenity, peace and space. Blue is cool. Blue is quality, blue blood, blue chip. Blue is horizon, nostalgia and expectations of those blue yonders. Out of the blue comes inspiration or disaster. Blue is mouldy, blue is cold and when we get the blues we're really down.

YELLOW   Yellow is sunshine, summer and growth. A warm colour, yellow (like red) has conflicting symbolism. It can mean happiness and joy but also cowardice and deceit. It is highly visible and is often used for hazard warnings and emergency vehicles. Yellow is cheerful. For years yellow ribbons were worn as a sign of hope as women waited for their men to come marching home from war.

BLACK   Black is associated with power, elegance, formality, death, evil and mystery. Black is a mysterious colour associated with fear and the unknown (black holes). It often has negative connotations (blacklist, black humour, black death). Black denotes strength and authority; it is considered to be a very formal, elegant and prestigious colour. Black creates a sense of perspective, depth and texture.

ORANGE   Orange combines the energy of red and the happiness of yellow. It is associated with joy, sunshine and the tropics. Orange represents enthusiasm, fascination, happiness, creativity, determination, attraction, success, encouragement and stimulation. A hot colour, orange radiates the sensation of heat.

GREEN   Green is the colour of the natural environment. It symbolizes growth, harmony, freshness and fertility. Green has a strong emotional correspondence with ecology. Dark green is also commonly associated with money. Green has great healing power. It is the most restful colour for the human eye; it can improve vision. Green suggests stability and endurance. Sometimes, green denotes lack of experience. Green, as opposed to red, means safety, and is the colour of 'go' in road traffic systems.

PURPLE   Purple combines the stability of blue and the energy of red. Purple is associated with royalty. It symbolizes power, nobility, luxury, and ambition. It conveys wealth and extravagance. Purple is associated with wisdom, dignity, independence, creativity, mystery and magic.

WHITE   White is associated with light, goodness, innocence, purity and virginity. It is considered to be the colour of perfection. White means safety, purity and cleanliness. As opposed to black, white usually has a positive connotation. As oppose to black in Western cultures, white symbolizes death in Eastern cultures.

3
Coloured wires as inspiration.
This photograph contains many
possible ways in which you can
translate colour. In the foreground,
the wires suggest coloured
line drawings, whilst the back
area could be investigated using
collage materials.

3

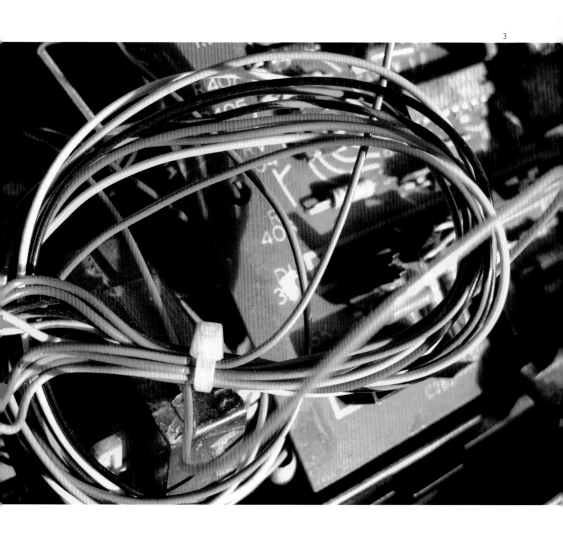

WHAT IS COLOUR?

Colour in design can be very subjective. With
the naked eye, we can see in the region of 350,000
colours. However, the scientific theory behind
colour is an extensive subject in its own right: the
logic of colour in terms of its hue, saturation, tones
and shade can be understood using pre-arranged
sequences and systems. Scientifically, colour
is simply pure light, made up of the colours that
we see when light is fractured, as in a rainbow or
through a prism. Colour is divided into three
main primary colours of red, yellow and blue,
and three secondary colours of orange, green and
purple. These are then further sub-divided into
tertiary colours that are mixtures of all of the
above in certain orders. Colour wheels, as seen in
graphic computer software, are useful to examine
the mixtures of colour that can be made.

In addition to understanding the basic colour
models, it is important for the textile designer to
remember that colour will appear differently when
on fabric, to how it appears on screen.

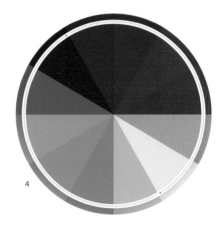

4

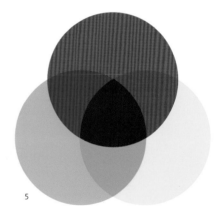

5

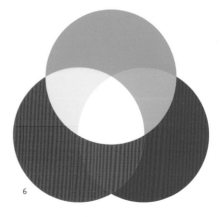

6

4
The colour wheel, made up
of primary, secondary and
tertiary colours.

5
The additive primaries. When
light is reflected (such as in print),
colour is created by the three
primaries cyan, magenta and
yellow. When these three colours
overlap, black is created.

6
The subtractive primaries. When
light is emitted (such as from
screens), colour is created by
the three primaries red, green
and blue. When all these colours
overlap, white light is created.

COLOUR DEFINITIONS

HUE   Hue means colour. When a colour is at its strongest and has not been diluted with black or white, it is at its purest. When mixed with another colour of the same intensity, it remains at its strongest.

SATURATION   Saturation in colour refers to its intensity. A highly saturated colour contains no white and is made up of a pure colour.

CHROMA   Another word used to describe the saturation or intensity of a colour.

MONOCHROME   When only one colour is being used, we call this working in monochrome. This is where a single colour is used, exploiting all the tones available within it.

TONE   Tone refers to the degree of lightness or darkness of colour, varying from the bright white of a light source through to shades of grey to the deepest black. How we perceive the tone of a colour also depends on its actual surface and texture. Value and shade are also used to describe tone.

TINTS   Tints are shades of colour and are usually pale in nature, containing a large proportion of white.

COLOUR PALETTE   A colour palette is a group of colours that have been identified together within a design.

'Look! Who says that there are only colours? There are also shades!'
DIANA VREELAND

COLOUR-GENERATING EXERCISE

Try mixing together red, yellow and blue. What do you get? You will probably have some kind of grey. When all the colours of the rainbow are mixed together with paint it becomes grey because no pigment is pure enough to become white, which is the pure light that colour is. Try mixing together different quantities of primary colours and add white to see what you get. See if you can create interesting shades of grey without using black.

7
Student's work using a range of mark making and colour techniques to create dynamic colour surface interest.

8
A collection of coloured textile fabrics. In–depth observation and analysis of colour is crucial for developing research that contains enough breadth of ideas for creating textile fabric collections.

OBSERVING AND ANALYZING COLOUR

As with pattern, structure, texture and surface, we rarely see one element in total isolation. Colour needs to be observed and analyzed in relation to other elements that are present where they will have an impact on the intensity, purity and quality of the colour. Texture will create different densities of colour within a surface, while pattern will create repetition and variation of colour. Surface may transform colour through reflective light; structure again will transform colour by creating different perspectives, which will affect the quality of colour. All of these must be considered if your research for textiles is to be highly visual and creative.

Analyzing colour has to be one of your paramount concerns. As discussed earlier, we see thousands of different colours with the naked eye and our job as textile designers is to reflect this enormous range of colour available to us. A Pantone shade or the colour of a crayon or gouache is a generic colour. Everybody can have access to that particular pigment or shade. Your job is to use it in a creative way to reflect the colour that you see with your own eyes.

Paint should always be blended unless there is a reason for using colour directly from the tube. Making up your own palette may take time but will create your own bespoke colour range that only you can replicate. Take time to do this whilst constantly observing and analyzing the colours in front of you.

8

9

10

The surface of the cloth usually refers to pattern, colour and motifs that have been applied through mixed media and print techniques. In order to successfully apply these, all the key areas of pattern, colour, texture and surface must be considered in relation to one another, as it is the combination of these key elements that determines the success of the surface design. Within textile design, the desired outcome is a successful composition that fully integrates the key areas so that the effect on the viewer is one of balance and harmony.

9
These student textile samples show how a range of surface effects can be created using stitching and knitting techniques. Investigating different surfaces is fundamental during research for textiles.

10
Inspiration for surface effects within drawing can be found all around us. This photograph, taken on a beach in winter, shows how sand particles and smooth stone can produce inspiration for surface research.

'Surface can mean texture, the outer layer, a membrane. Through the surface can mean something emerging or beyond the immediately visible.'
LESLEY MILLAR

WHAT DO WE MEAN BY SURFACE?

Surface in textile design refers in the main to the image, pattern or decorative elements placed on top of the cloth's exterior. A surface design can be applied using both flat, two-dimensional techniques, such as hand or digital printing, or through a combination of applied techniques, such as mixed media and collage. Increasingly in this area, the boundaries between graphics, illustration, product and textiles are merging, where a surface design can be easily transferred from one type of surface to another. This provides exciting possibilities for textile designers as new types of materials and surfaces can be used. Surface techniques within textiles have therefore opened new possibilities for designers where restrictions of materials are no longer a limitation. As designers Linda Florence on pages 66–67, and Johanna Basford on pages 84–87 demonstrate, students and graduates of textile design courses are now able to position themselves as surface designers, developing new types of practice for those with a background in textile design.

11

12

11
Textile graduate Kirsty Fenton's work illustrates how different surfaces can bring meaning and narrative to textiles. This work uses stitching and fabric to convey a sense of loss, that so many children in developing nations experience.

12
The animal horns in this photograph provide a great source for researching natural surfaces. Carefully analyze the surface texture and try to describe this visually, as a scientist would through a microscope.

MARK-MAKING EXERCISE

Mark making is a method you can use to create different types of surface interest on paper. These techniques are a great starting point for investigating surface pattern. Using simple drawing tools, often using found objects such as feathers, sticks, scourers and sponges, numerous surfaces can be created easily and quickly.

On a large A2 (C) sheet of paper, draw out three rows of 10cm × 10cm (3.9" × 3.9") squares with a space between each square. Using black and white only, create different surface patterns in each square using a range of found materials. Materials could include all sorts of domestic objects such as sponges, toothbrushes, wire brushes and pastry cutters. Also source natural found objects such as twigs, feathers, fir cones and shells, to name just a few.

Using black ink, try and create as many different surface patterns as possible. Experiment with printing, spotting, drawing, flicking, stamping, masking and spraying. Experiment with masking fluid and tape to block areas off. Use resist materials such as wax and crayon. Don't labour over each one, spend only a few minutes on each. At the end of this exercise you should have a sheet with a wide variety of surface patterns. Keep this sheet as a reference point for creating different surfaces to use as part of your drawing material. Write a comment beside each one to remind yourself of the tools and materials you used.

13

13
Worn, rusted and corroded
surfaces such as seen here can
provide visual references in
surface, together with colour,
texture and pattern.

AUTHOR TIP

When you are out on
location, try and record
as much information
as possible. You may not
be able to re-visit and
it's important that you
have enough information
to start developing your
design drawings.

SURFACE TECHNIQUES

Hand surface research techniques can include the following:

STAMPING   This is where force or pressure is applied to a surface to create an image, motif or decorative element to the surface of the material. Often, the force applied can be used to create differences in the surface's thickness. Traditionally, this technique has been used in many different cultures, where the simple process of repetitive stamping of an image onto a surface can create numerous surface effects.

PRINTING   Printing techniques are synonymous with creating surface interest. From digital graphic imagery generated through photography to low-tech techniques using hand stencils, sponging and block printing, a base material can be transformed.

COLLAGING   By using a range of different types of materials to create imagery and pattern through collage, a surface can be developed with tactile qualities. You might, for example, sew onto your surface, or scratch into it using sharp tools.

SURFACE EFFECTS EXERCISE

Create a two-dimensional surface using scraps of materials such as coloured transparent tissue papers, photographs and recycled materials such as old labels, tickets or wrappers and corrugated paper, to create different surfaces for drawing.

Or, using a plain sheet of white paper, choose two or three actions from the following list to create different surface effects: layering, ripping, scratching, washing, creasing, pleating, folding, rubbing, slashing.

14

When it comes to structure, most of your visual research will be concerned with how to capture its essential qualities in two-dimensional drawings. Textiles have often been used to portray an illusion of structural forms on fabric which, when draped, give an impression of depth, space, scale and proportion. Digital print in textiles can also create flat images of interesting structures that play with our visual senses.

'When it comes to structure, it is a challenge to try to pull the image out of the painting and the three dimensions.'

AURA WILMING

14
Laser-cut fabrics by Rachel Haddon create open work constructions which, as seen here, can use space, light and structure simultaneously.

15
Structure can be easily found in the built environment. Here, a student examines different architectural structures and explores the relationship between different building structures through line drawing and collage.

15

16

17

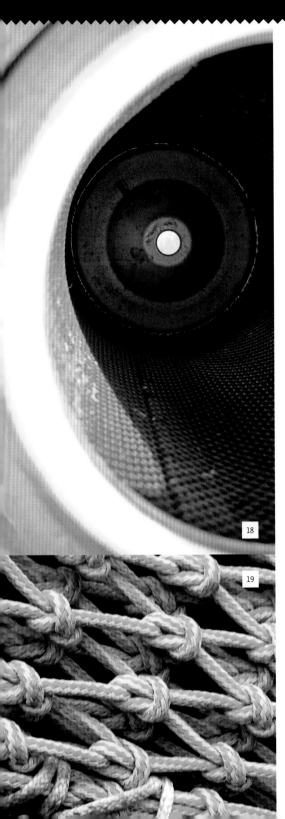

Structural inspiration can come from many places. Here is a list of some you may wish to consider.

NATURAL ENVIRONMENT   Trees, bushes, flowers, ploughed fields, haystacks, rocks, farm buildings, vegetable patches, tractor-tyre prints, landscapes, seascapes, rock pools, animal skeletons, living creatures and the medical world.

BUILT ENVIRONMENT   Scaffolding, building sites, scrap merchants, shopping aisles, buildings, fencing, pylons, CCTV cameras, aerials, cranes, circuitboards, engines, sculptures, ceramics, domestic products and columns.

16
Natural flotsam on a beach. Structure and form can be clearly observed in this photograph.

17
Cut patterned metalwork provides a source of inspiration for creating illusion, space and depth for printed textiles.

18
Structural perspective, texture and pattern are all visually accessible within this cylindrical object.

19
Structure in objects such as this knotted fishing net immediately lends itself to research investigation for constructed textiles.

OBSERVING AND
ANALYZING STRUCTURE

Structures come in many different forms. Some are soft, others are hard; we are surrounded by utilitarian, functional and also highly decorative and patterned structures. Depending on the type of textiles you are creating, you will need to capture different types of visual information.

For constructed textiles, you might consider the actual three-dimensional construction aspects of the structure. What materials have been used? What can this tell you about the types of materials you might use? What lies behind the surface? What about the form, the texture, the light reflected?

For surface and printed textiles, proportion, perspective, line, pattern and composition may be more relevant where a two-dimensional representation is the ultimate goal.

Here we will consider some of the structures that you may wish to incorporate within your visual research.

THE BODY   Life drawing helps us to observe the body as a three-dimensional form and analyze the shapes within and the space around the body. Drawing the body is useful for understanding softer structures, the skeletal framework and movement of limbs. Through studying the structure of the body, we can begin to make decisions about the best approach for designing textiles for the body. Drawing animal skeletal structures is another great source. Museums containing ornithology and mammal collections are ideal locations for investigating structures.

ARCHITECTURE   Unlike the body, architecture provides hard, static structures which can be used as an inspirational source for drawing. Modern buildings tend to consist of state-of-the-art materials where glass and concrete are often the most predominant. Classical architecture provides more decorative qualities, where stone-carving patterns, wooden entrances and wrought ironwork provide a different stimulus. Within every city centre, we see an array of examples of architecture. When researching architecture, it is important to remember to consider buildings under construction – even the scaffolding and exposure of the interior can provide additional structural sources.

CHAOTIC STRUCTURES   Many structures around us are not organized or designed. They do, however, provide exciting examples of chaotic structures. Dishes piled up in the sink, a jumble sale, a scrapyard and a cycle repair shop are just some examples of where you may find more random types of structures to draw from.

20
Stephanie Szumlakowski's
crocheted sample uses elasticated
yarn to create structure.

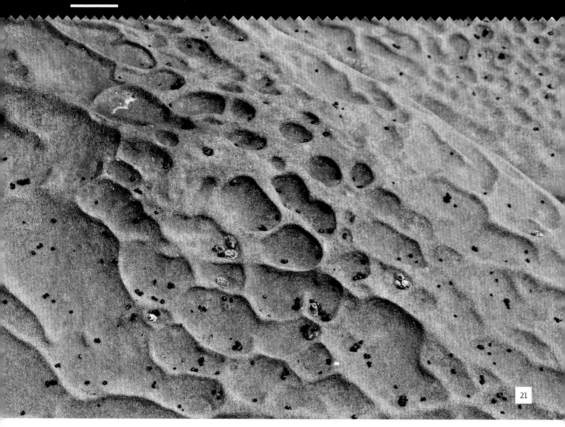

21

Texture manifests itself through its tactile and its visual qualities to convey a range of messages and emotions. Different textures evoke different types of responses. Some surfaces invite touch, while others are repellent and so are the textures that suggest those surfaces. Most textures have a naturalistic quality where they repeat a motif in a random way. With a texture, you may be aware of the repeating motif but you are more aware of the surface.

'Textures are a way of representing the union of two feelings: view and touch.'
NANI MARQUINA

21
Texture on sand leaves a physical memory of the wave's motion. This ephemeral texture continually changes with the tide. Try and capture this texture through a range of different media, such as photography, wash and ink, line drawing and collage.

22
The texture of a corroded metal base. In your drawing, try to capture the fragility of the metal as it begins to flake away from the surface. Use different types of materials and media to reflect the different textural elements here, such as shellac, tissue papers and foils.

23
Tree bark creates a range of different textured layers similar to contour maps. Consider building up textural surfaces by using papers with different thicknesses to create your own contour map.

24
Peeling paint creates an organic texture similar to natural lichens and fungi. This photograph shows a strong contrast between the background wall colour and the peeling paint. Carefully analyze the textural colour variations and use a range of different materials and media to convey both the colour and textural qualities.

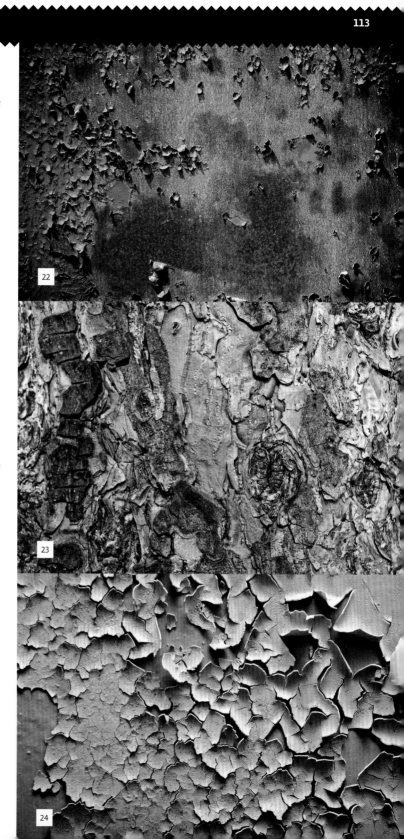

'The best way to get a good idea is to get a lot of ideas.'

LINUS PAULING

TACTILE TEXTURE

Tactile means touch. Tactile texture refers to the feel of a surface. This quality is a primary concern when designing textiles that will be worn or felt. The actual surface texture needs to be felt, or seen with light across its surface to make the texture visible. Collages are an effective way of investigating the textural qualities of your visual sources. Textured paper and other three-dimensional textural materials can be used to make a tactile surface, for example.

VISUAL TEXTURE

Visual texture refers to the illusion of the surface's texture. It is concerned with how a tactile texture looks. Consider, for example, how a photograph captures visual textures. No matter how rough objects in the photograph look, the surface of the photograph is smooth and flat. Visual texture is always present because everything has a surface and therefore a texture. When photographs are used as collage materials, texture starts to take on more importance. Here you can use the illusion of many different textures, together with colour and imagery in your drawing. Collage can be a useful drawing method by which you can develop a rich variety of colours, textures and images as part of your research for textiles.

Both types are important to the designer: visual texture is more apparent in two-dimensional printed textiles, whilst tactile texture is mainly used in knitted, woven and mixed-media textiles.

25
This page from a student sketchbook explores a number of textures in relation to one another. The student is able to analyze the different textural surfaces and work simultaneously across textures, integrating other elements such as structure, colour and pattern within their drawing.

'Texture adds variety and visual stimulus to the surface of a painting.'

BRITTON FRANCIS

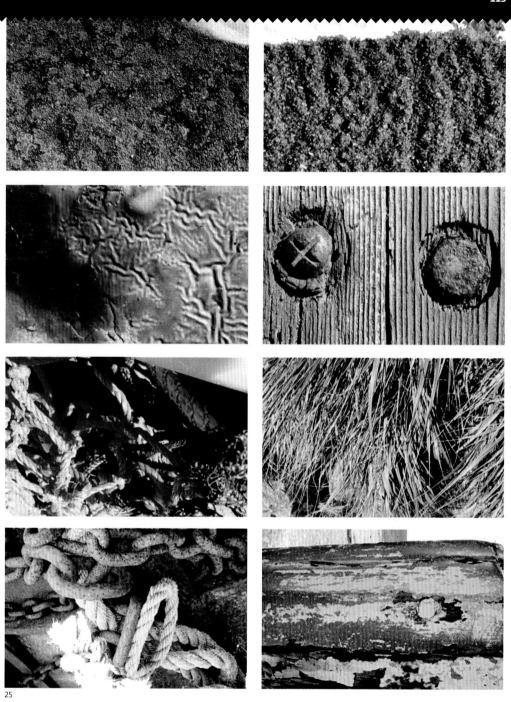

25

TEXTURE AND PATTERN

Texture and pattern are related. When you look closely at an object, such as a tree, you can see the pattern of leaves that make its surface. When you back away, you lose the awareness of the leaves and instead notice the texture that the leaves make on the tree. As you move further away still, you can see the pattern of the trees making up the forest and finally the texture of the forest itself. In this way, pattern and structure become apparent.

TEXTURE AND STRUCTURE

Variation and inconsistency across materials can create texture. For example, by using varying widths and thicknesses of materials and line, a physical variance can be created from a mono-chrome drawing. There is no need to use colour. Constructed textiles, particularly weave, rely on techniques such as this when choosing the different weights, thicknesses and types of fibre and yarn to use.

26
Texture and pattern are interlinked here; whether looking at the bluebell carpet or the pattern and colour of the branches and trees. Try to look at your surroundings both close up and from a distance. By doing this, you will notice different types of textures and patterns emerging within the same location.

26

27

27
A collection of espadrilles
outside a shop in Spain.
Wherever you are, remember to
capture examples of different
textures. When observing the
textures, look at the relationship
between them, for example the
brick wall and the door frame
together with the rubber and rope
soles of the espadrilles.

28

TEXTURE AND EMOTION

Individuals react both psychologically and emotionally to texture. Feelings of elegance and sophistication can be evoked through luxurious materials such as velvet, for example, or strong masculine emotions with leather. We can manipulate textural qualities and use materials in a contradictory fashion to elicit a mix of emotional responses. Smooth textures are often less obtrusive, undemanding and may be understated enough to enable other elements such as colour and pattern to be more dominant.

Rough textures tend to attract more attention, but can also overshadow the use of other elements within a design. A textural softness begs to be touched or cuddled. It is friendly, cosy and inviting. Softness need not always portray a feminine or childlike response though, it can also be used to convey more difficult and challenging ideas in a less threatening way. Freddie Robbins' knitted 'Homes of Crime' (on page 72) shows how this can be done.

'Make me a fabric
that looks like poison.'
ISSEY MIYAKE

28
Textures can convey deep emotions. In this student work, the feather imagery, together with the oily texture, creates conflicting emotions and themes, such as opulence, death and phobias.

29

30

PRINTS & GRAPHICS   NEW FRACTALS

PHICS

Most of us see pattern as a collection of forms, lines, symbols, tones and colours. How you observe and analyze pattern as a textile designer during your initial research stage is fundamental to how the pattern will be developed into a textile design. Pattern is rarely observed in isolation and can be identified, recorded and analyzed through the lens of the other key themes identified in this book: colour, surface, structure and texture. Therefore, throughout your research, look for patterns of colour, patterns of structure and patterns within surfaces and textures.

In order to make pattern and become a pattern-maker, you must first begin to recognize it around you within the environment. Understanding and using pattern is an essential part of being a textile designer as it is you, the pattern-maker and designer who gives pattern its purpose. To fully understand the use of pattern, we will explore the different types of pattern found around us and within textiles. This will enable an understanding of how to find pattern and use it within design.

'If pattern has a secret ingredient it lies in the skill with which the pattern-maker employs a few visual strat egies...the principles of repetition and variation.'
WILLIAM JUSTEMA

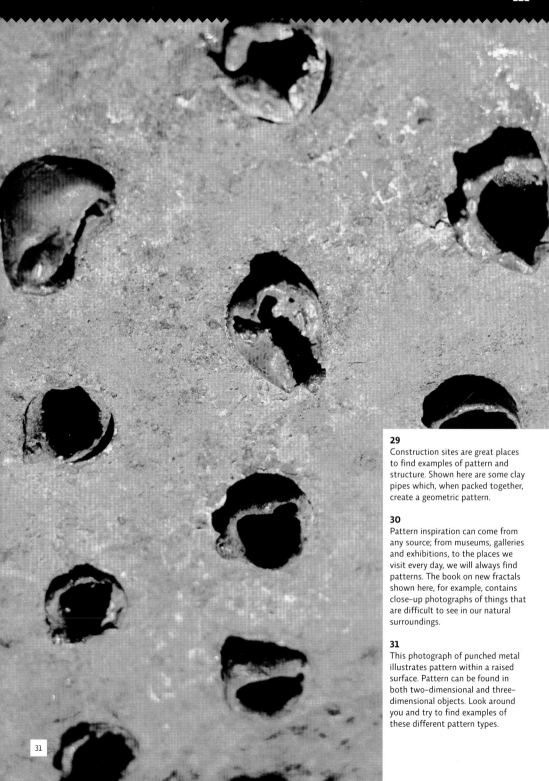

29
Construction sites are great places to find examples of pattern and structure. Shown here are some clay pipes which, when packed together, create a geometric pattern.

30
Pattern inspiration can come from any source; from museums, galleries and exhibitions, to the places we visit every day, we will always find patterns. The book on new fractals shown here, for example, contains close–up photographs of things that are difficult to see in our natural surroundings.

31
This photograph of punched metal illustrates pattern within a raised surface. Pattern can be found in both two–dimensional and three–dimensional objects. Look around you and try to find examples of these different pattern types.

31

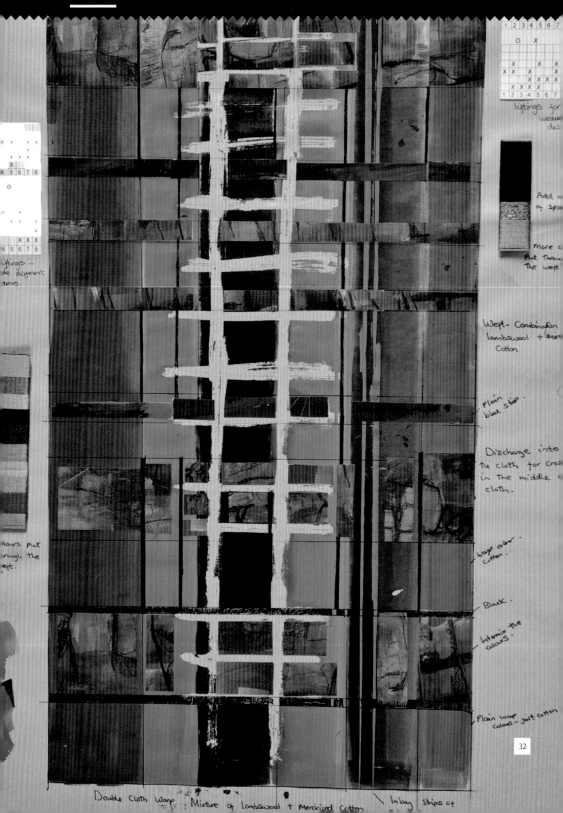

WHAT IS PATTERN?

Pattern is used extensively in textile design, from surface printing to patterns created through the structure of woven and knitted cloth. It is most often used in an aesthetic way; to appeal to the senses, to be beautiful, engaging, soft, comforting, radical or visionary. Therefore, it is a sensorial experience for the viewer or user, and the designer must employ their knowledge and skill to make patterns to serve this purpose.

Pattern has its roots in nature and designers of all descriptions often use nature as their source of inspiration – the zoologist D'Arcy Thompson and architect Peter Stevens explain that nature uses the same five pattern structures continuously. These are:

BRANCHING Think of how the arteries in your body grow and expand or how trees grow from their roots to their outer branches. Branching patterns are seen regularly in textile design, where rooted motifs spread across the fabric surface or are constructed to form the whole.

'An age without good pattern is an age that does not look at nature carefully.'
SOETSU YANAGI

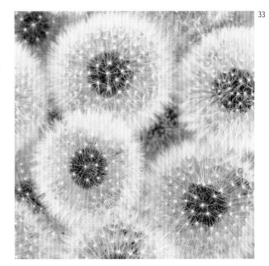

33

34

32
This drawing for weave shows how pattern is an integral part of the process of creating textiles. Here, the designer has visually 'mapped out' their weave pattern with wrappings of yarn, together with the lifting and warp pattern that will be used to create the design.

33
Dandelion heads illustrate 'explosions', one of the five pattern structures discussed here. The explosion pattern refers to the spotting and floating pattern motifs used in textile design.

34
This image shows how branch formations have been organized into a pattern.

'In matters of visual form we sense that nature plays favourites. Among her darlings are spirals, meanders, branching patterns and 120-degree joints...nature acts like a producer who brings on the same players each night in different costumes for different roles.'

PETER STEVENS

36

37

35

38

MEANDERS   The meander is a wandering line like a long winding river. It can be smooth and sleek and single or there can be lots of them together, giving an impression of movement. If straightened out, we have stripes. Repeating stripes is one of the simplest and most common repeat structures, particularly for knitted and woven textiles. Inspiration for stripes can be seen all around us – from clothes hanging on a clothes rail to the reflection of a landscape in water. We are surrounded by stripe structures wherever we go. Although in essence a straightforward format, getting the right balance between stripe proportions, colour contrasts and surface texture requires painstaking research. The fashion company Missoni have over many years built up their brand essentially based on stripe patterns, which can then be translated into knitwear, accessories and interiors (see pages 150–151).

BUBBLES   Think of the way a corn on the cob has bubbles sticking side by side or the way in which soap bubbles in a bathtub stick and multiply. Bubble formations create texture as well as pattern.

EXPLOSIONS   Imagine a drop of water hitting a table or a dandelion head as it is about to burst from its central point. The explosion pattern is used extensively in textiles and is often recognized as simple spotted motifs or free-floating forms across the design.

SPIRALS   Spirals are one of the most culturally prominent symbols and they reflect different meanings in nearly every culture. The spiral represented eternity within Celtic culture, for example. Spirals can be found in many natural phenomena such as shells, pine cones and fern leaves. They are used extensively in textiles for their flowing and curvaceous properties.

When you look closely at the man-made environment, you will start to recognize how these five pattern structures have been used in many of our designed structures and surfaces, from architecture to textiles and graphics.

35
Soap bubbles describe this repeating pattern structure, where the rainbow colours give an additional element to the composition.

36
Spirals, most commonly seen in nature, are mimicked in the built environment, such as in the office building shown here.

37
Spirals are most commonly found in shells, where the pattern and structure opens out as it reaches the edges of the shell. Try and observe closely these formations in nature; from shells to unfolding ferns, no two are the same.

38
Meandering lines produce a striped pattern. The stripes are often not straight and in this image of magazine ends, they can bleed and appear blurred as the lines merge into one another.

39

MOTIFS

We understand pattern as the reccurence of similar forms at regular intervals: a stripe (meander), for example, or a bubble formation. However, these pattern structures require an ornamental form that is called a 'motif' and the way in which they occur within textile design is called 'the repeat'.

Identifying a motif that could lend itself to a repeat is an essential task for the designer. Within a pattern, we can identify a single motif or a collection of motifs that are then arranged as a pattern structure in such a way as to form the basis of the design. We can refer to the motif as the core element to the design of the pattern.

While gathering visual information, it is often helpful to find the central element or motif of a repeat. Often in nature, you will find patterns that have a central form or shape, varying to some degree in colour, texture, structure, and so on.

Try and observe these variations very carefully, however slight, to fully capture the essential qualities within the motif.

By carefully observing and analyzing these individual qualities within your motif at this initial stage, you will be able to develop your own personal visual language for design.

39
Drawing showing a bird motif by Carrie Ferguson. Further additional arrow motifs have been included in the design to create a pattern suggesting movement.

40
The repeating elements seen in the bird pattern have now been carefully placed to create an overall pattern.

40

41

REPEATS

As previously described, a pattern is created through the repeat of a motif or motifs. The use of a repeat pattern can be seen in all areas of textile design, from wall coverings and furnishing fabrics to the fashion catwalk. Repeat patterns are without doubt the staple design for textiles and really the 'bread and butter' for the textile industry. As a designer, an understanding of repeat is essential within all aspects of textile design and manufacture.

DISRUPTIVE PATTERNS

Disruptive patterns or camouflage patterns were originally used primarily by the military but have now been widely adopted for fashion wear. Disruptive Pattern Material (known as DPM) tends to be inspired by the natural world and is now increasingly used by designers for cultural references.

PATTERN-GENERATING EXERCISE

We have discussed the importance of pattern and some of the key components that make up pattern. In this exercise you need to think of yourself as a pattern searcher, identifying different types of pattern structures and finding the ornamental form or motif. Think of ways you might organize your motifs within some of nature's structures.

This could include looking at books on a shelf, tiles on a roof or pavement patterns. Try and find less obvious patterns where a repeat element is present. Once you have found your pattern structures, capture them through drawing or using a camera. Again, think of yourself as a visual detective, trying to gather as much information as possible by looking at pattern through colour, structure, surface and texture.

41
Repeating elements have been carefully placed to create this overall pattern by Carlene Edwards.

Yinka Shonibare is a British–Nigerian contemporary artist, currently working in London in the UK. Much of his work explores colonialism and post–colonialism through painting, sculpture, photography, film and performance. He frequently uses textiles in his creations, often using them to symbolize cultural, racial and sociological meaning. His work has been exhibited worldwide, including at the Brooklyn Museum, New York, USA, The Museum of African Art at the Smithsonian Institution, Washington DC, USA, and on the fourth plinth at Trafalgar Square in London, UK.

▶ **42**
CHA-CHA-CHA (1997)

A pair of women's shoes, covered in African-print fabric. By covering a pair of women's shoes in African print, Shonibare comments on the dance halls of the 1950s, an era which represented Africa's hope for Independence.

▶ **43**
LEISURE LADY WITH PUGS (2001)

A life-size mannequin with fibreglass dogs. The mannequin is dressed in Dutch wax print cotton. Shonibare explores race, class and colonialism using textiles and Afrian fabrics.

42

Tim Gresham works in woven tapestry and photography – two very different mediums that use similar ideas of structure and pattern. He is particularly drawn to the contrast between the two: the slow, methodical growth of a tapestry, and the instant, sometimes spontaneous capturing of a photograph.

HOW DID YOU GET STARTED?

I graduated with a Diploma of Creative Arts (Visual), from the Darling Downs Institute of Advanced Education, now the University of Southern Queensland. Then I spent five years weaving full time at the Australian Tapestry Workshop, where the weavers work in collaboration with established Australian (mostly) artists on large commissioned projects. Towards the end of 1992 I left the workshop and worked for a few years with a small collective of tapestry weavers, exhibiting together and producing large-scale works. Since around 1995 I have been working in my own practice, which is financially supported by my photography work; this mostly involves photographing artwork for other artists.

WHERE DO YOU WORK?

For the last 12 years I have been working in a large studio complex in Collingwood, an inner suburb of Melbourne. It is an old warehouse/factory over two levels and a basement, divided into spaces of varying sizes. Some lockable and others open. A range of people rent the spaces, from young artists and craftspeople just out of university to fashion designers, architects and photographers. There is even an acting school in one of the larger spaces. Around 90 people do some sort of work in the building.

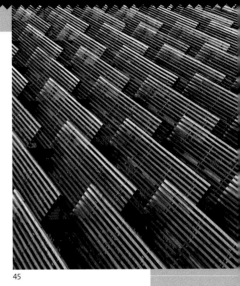

45

WHAT IS THE ENVIRONMENT LIKE IN YOUR STUDIO?

My studio is open and very light and airy. Because my section of the studios is open plan, I have excellent natural light from both my windows and those on the other side of the building. Despite the large amount of people using the studios my section is quiet most of the time, as my nearest neighbours don't use the space full time.

CAN YOU TELL ME ABOUT YOUR DESIGN PROCESS? HOW DO YOU GENERATE IDEAS?

My design process varies depending on the body of work, but generally a starting point will be my photographs. Always working from black and white photographs, so as to concentrate solely on the forms and patterns, I usually do some drawings abstracting the images to find a suitable idea to weave, while constantly thinking about the qualities and techniques of tapestry weaving and the limitations involved. This is often a very slow part of the process as I am always

44

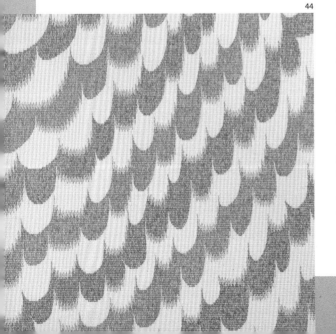

trying to find the simplest solution, keeping in mind the techniques I'll use. But the most important thing is that I come up with an idea where the weaving process itself flows freely and is enjoyable. Once a body of work is in progress, the ideas themselves often flow freely and evolve from piece to piece and even to and fro from tapestry to photography. Drawing the designs loosely by hand causes the shapes and patterns of my tapestries to vary, and sometimes instead of using a cartoon, I draw the design directly on the warp as the tapestry progresses. This organic spontaneity contrasts nicely with the precise mathematical structure of the weave. If I am doing a series of large tapestries I will sometimes weave small samples or maquettes first, to consolidate the ideas and exhibit them with the larger works.

WHY DO YOU RESEARCH? WHY IS IT IMPORTANT?

Research is for gathering images and consolidating ideas. Part of the research is looking at other artists' work that has a similar aesthetic to my own. This helps to refine my ideas and the direction of my work. I think it is important to look at both earlier artists as well your contemporaries and try to get a sense of where you fit in your artistic community.

WHAT ARE YOUR MAIN SOURCES OF RESEARCH?

My main source of research would have to be my photography. I can spend hours looking through my old photos, picking out a selection to draw from. Or I'll wander into the city with a camera for some fresh images and check out a few galleries at the same time. And if there is a particular artist I want to look at, then it's the good old Google search.

WHAT OR WHO HAS HAD THE MOST INFLUENCE ON YOUR WORK?

I think the most influence has been modernist art, design and architecture. To name a few artists, I like the work of Bridget Riley, Mark Rothko and Jeffrey Smart's cool, still, urban landscapes. Some inspiration comes from tapestry weavers, to name just a few, Archie Brennan, Susan Martin Maffei, numerous British weavers, and my colleague and friend Sara Lindsay. And of course photographers, among many, Bill Brandt, Henri Cartier-Bresson, Edward and Brett Weston, Bill Henson, the list is almost endless. Living in

Melbourne, much of the inspiration for my ideas comes from my local environment; a combination of imagery from the city, and colour from the surrounding landscape.

WHAT IS YOUR GREATEST ACHIEVEMENT TO DATE?

I think my greatest achievement was being selected as a finalist in the Cicely and Colin Rigg Contemporary Design Award at the National Gallery of Victoria in 2003. The large work I produced for this exhibition has recently been acquired by Ararat Regional Gallery for their collection specializing in contemporary textiles.

DO YOU HAVE ANY ADVICE TO THOSE THINKING OF A CAREER IN TEXTILE DESIGN?

I don't really think of myself as a textile designer, more a textile artist/craftsperson, but I think it is important to try to have a good idea about where you are going with your work. Also to realize that sometimes that direction has to change, and even a small change can be quite significant.

44
'Frequency IV',
2008. 60cm × 60cm (23" × 23")

45
'Liquid Module III', 2008.
60cm × 60cm (23" × 23")

46
'Maquette XIII', 2009.
15cm × 15cm (6" × 6")

'There are no rules, only tools.'
GLENN VILPPU

1

6

TECHNIQUES FOR OBSERVATIONAL DRAWING

Drawing for textile design is often misunderstood. Many see it as a chore which must be completed before the 'real' work of design can begin. Drawing, however, is fundamental to the design process and instrumental in providing a rich source of material on which a design can be based.

Traditional techniques for drawing are not always the most relevant and you should develop your own individual style of drawing to create your own personal signature.

1
Student sketchbook – observational drawing of vintage sewing machines. The student uses predominately line drawing with smudged pastel and paint to understand the three–dimensional structure through drawing.

2

There is no 'right' way to draw. Some people are very good at observational or 'realistic' drawing, where their understanding of proportion, scale and composition provides a very accurate representation of their subject. This doesn't, however, necessarily mean that they are good textile designers.

Drawing is essentially about ideas, testing things out, experimenting and trying to visualize from a wide range of approaches. Drawing is a dynamic and highly creative process and ultimately the backbone to all of your design work.

A LIST OF PRIMARY MATERIALS FOR DRAWING

Pencils: 8B, 6B, 4B, 2B, HB

Small pencil sharpener

Charcoal pencils: 6B, 2B, white

Compressed charcoal, several sticks

Vine charcoal – soft, several sticks

Rubbers: kneaded and vinyl

Pastels

Wax crayons

Gouache

Watercolours

India ink, black and assorted colours

Drawing ink – sepia or burnt umber

Penholder and nibs (one must have a point for drawing)

Several bristled brushes – large and small

Fixative (optional)

Masking tape

Fingers!

WASH AND INK

Wash and ink is a very simple technique. It creates a range of spontaneous marks, strokes and lines made by ink or pens that essentially 'bleed' with the wet surface.

Firstly, wet your paper surface with water. You can use a sponge for this, or paint it on with a large brush. Next, using a pen tip dipped in ink, or similar (maybe even a stick or a feather), start to draw onto the washed paper. The line of the ink will immediately start to run. Experiment with this technique and find ways to control the effect. You can do this in a number of ways. Change the type of paper surface – what happens if you use a watercolour paper compared with cartridge paper? Try saturating the paper in different degrees to control the bleeding. Also experiment with having some areas of the paper washed and others not.

You can also use wash techniques such as 'discharge', where the colour is taken out by the 'wash'. Try painting over with ink and then drawing with bleach.

2
Wash and ink techniques, as shown here, provide a spontaneous and unexpected aspect to drawing. Experiment with different 'found' tools such as sticks and feathers, to explore different wash effects.

3

USING PAINT AND PENCIL

You will be familiar with using some types
of paint. Gouache and watercolours are commonly
used by designers as they are quick to dry,
easy to mix and retain great colour. Working with
more than one type of media at the same time,
however, requires a slightly different approach –
both need to work and complement each other.
Try drawing your subject with a pencil line first.
Using a wash of paint, you will see the pencil line
coming through under the surface. Next, experiment
with using both pencil line and paint to describe
your composition.

'There is something magical in
seeing what you can do, what
texture and tone and colour
you can produce merely with a
pen point and a bottle of ink.'
IDA RENTOUL OUTHWAITE

SPONGING AND SCRATCHING

Sponging is a technique used for applying paint using a sponge. Large uneven surfaces can be covered and exciting effects can be created. Try using a white wall emulsion paint, which is relatively inexpensive, with a sponge. Once the surface has dried or a crust has formed over the paint surface, you can start to 'scratch' into the paint's surface. A wide range of tools can be used for this – try using sticks, a scalpel, a pencil or even a pin.

3
A student sketchbook page investigating architectural structures through paint and pencil.

4
An example from a student's drawing, showing how paint has been applied thickly using a sponge and then scratched into to create a surface relief.

4

DRAWING WITH STITCH

A sewing machine can also be used as a drawing tool. By removing the sewing foot, you can begin to 'free-stitch' to create unusual lines. Try using the sewing machine without any thread. Hold your paper up to the light to see the effect that the holes have made on the paper. If you don't have a sewing machine, try stitching paper by hand with a sewing needle. Experiment with pulling the thread to create gathered or ruffled textured areas within your drawing.

5
This example of felt and embroidery shows how stitch can be used as a drawing tool.

6
In this example, a student has used stitch directly onto paper to create irregular lines and raised surface interest.

7
An example of combining a range of mark-making techniques – wash and ink with smudged charcoal and line.

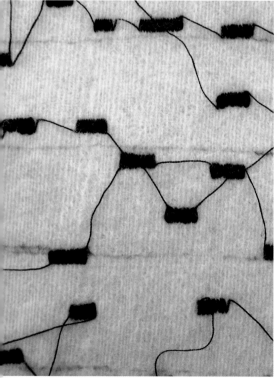

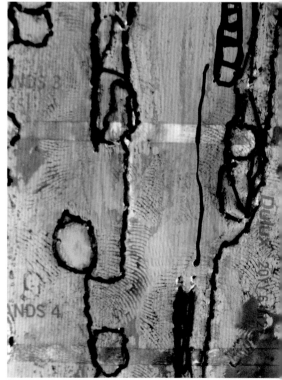

5   6

7

MAKING MARKS

As previously mentioned, mark making plays
an important role in creating dynamic surface
effects that can then be translated into textiles.
Many of the techniques detailed can be used
to create a range of spontaneous marks on paper
or other surfaces.

8

DRAWING EXERCISE

Firstly, select some objects to observe. Rather than trying to anticipate what your drawing may look like using particular objects, try to choose objects that have some meaning or narrative. Arrange these objects close together, perhaps on their side or upside down or on top of each other. Next make a viewer by cutting out a 4cm × 4cm (1.5" × 1.5") window from the centre of an A4 (A (letter)) sheet of paper. Start to move your window around your objects, looking for an interesting composition.

8
These observational drawings were made on location in a park using pencil and paints. Each quick sketch here provides different information which can be further developed back in the studio.

Using large sheets of paper, preferably A1 (D), you are now ready to create a series of quick, dynamic drawings, each time using a different media. These might include: permanent marker, pencil, graphite stick, biro, fine liner, large brush, wax crayon, charcoal and so on. Try to stand while drawing as this will increase your range of movement and arm extension. Work on the drawing exercises directly over the top of one another using the same piece of paper. Change your view finder position and rotate your paper between each exercise.

DRAWING FROM MEMORY

Look carefully at your objects for two minutes – try and capture in your mind the shapes of the objects together in your composition view finder. Cover up the objects and now draw from your memory.

CONTINUOUS LINE DRAWING

Draw your subject, keeping your eyes on the subject matter the whole time. You must keep your pen in contact with the

Try enlarging your work by taping your drawing tool to the end of a long stick. You'll need to put your paper on the floor and rearrange the position of your objects – again, limit your time.

Repeat all of these exercises with differing media overlapping on the page. The timed, fast pace of the exercise should help you to observe quickly and produce fast and dynamic drawing.

It is vital that you review the drawings you have made. Using masking tape, paper windows or your camera, identify areas of interest. This might be the varying quality of marks, the composition or the new structures that have been made. Remember that this is all part of the drawing process.

The boundaries between design disciplines are becoming increasingly blurred. We see textile designers today working with many other types of materials. This offers new exciting possibilities and observational drawing techniques using mixed media are particularly useful in triggering new approaches to textiles.

Mixed media refers to the process of combining two or more types of media to create a single composition. This technique for observational drawing enables many different surfaces and textures to be made. Found objects can be used in combination with traditional drawing media, such as paints and pencils.

Mixed media extends the experience of drawing through the use of line, tone, texture, shape and form, using traditional materials together with other types of media such as collage, paint, paper structures and wire, investigating composition in two dimensions and in relief.

Some commonly used mixed–media techniques are outlined here.

COLLAGE

Collage is a technique used for assembling different types of materials together. A collage can include all sorts of materials, such as newspaper and magazine clippings, coloured and handmade papers, photographs, postcards and many other found objects.

'Things have really moved on a lot. The materials I use range from wood and paper to plastics and metal.'
KAREN NICOL

COLLAGE EXERCISE

Gather together a range of found paper-based materials. These might include used envelopes and stamps, cardboard, old dress patterns, maps, newspaper, bus tickets or shopping receipts.

Using an A2 (C) sheet of paper, begin to assemble and glue your found objects whilst at the same time observing your composition (as for drawing techniques). Consider the shapes and forms of the objects and how they overlap. Rip, shred and cut paper edges to reflect the composition. This collage can then be further developed using traditional drawing materials to add detail and colour.

9
Student collage work using a range of found paper collage materials. Collage gives this working drawing a range of patterns and surface effects that can then be used to develop further drawings and design work.

10

RELIEF

Drawing in relief involves building up surfaces.
This can be achieved by creating raised areas
within a drawing through layering and overlapping
collage materials together. Consider using different
materials together, by layering tissue paper over
another surface, for example, the texture, print or
colour will appear through to the outer surface.

10
Student drawing using brown
paper and paint. The use of an
additional surface provides a
contrast in the depth and tone
of the colour to the drawing.

11
Student work using open
cut-work to create line patterns.
The effect of overlaying a number
of cut pieces gives the piece
additional depth.

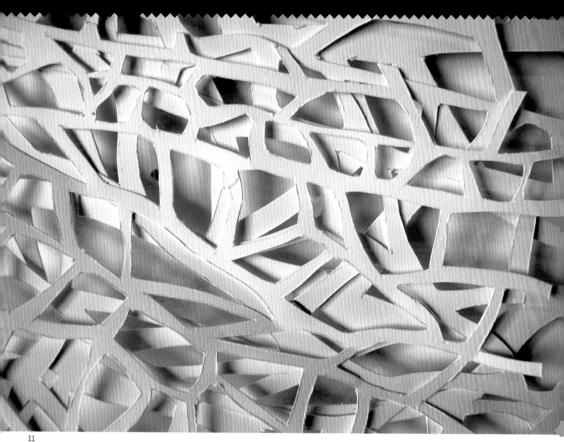

11

OBSERVING LINES

Investigating line within your composition can be done in a number of ways that don't always involve 'drawing' on a flat surface. Drawing using a sewing machine is one way of doing this. Wire can also be used to investigate the three-dimensional space. To do this, choose a pliable wire that can be easily bent and twisted.

Try also cutting into paper with a scalpel to create repetitive and patterned lines. This technique changes the handle and quality of the paper where it will begin to 'sag' or bend to create different relief effects.

AUTHOR TIP

Here are some ways to alter the quality of your paper: folding, bending, rolling, twisting, tearing, crumpling, cutting, shredding, puncturing, scoring, weaving, layering, slotting, mushing.

12

Scale can be used to investigate a subject from different perspectives. As mentioned previously, drawing for textile design is primarily concerned with investigating detail. This can be done through the surface, the pattern, the texture or the structure.

By zooming in on an area, you can examine the minutiae, as a scientist would do, of the subject. You may, however, want to observe and record this on a completely different scale. You can do this in a number of ways. Firstly, you can draw what we are seeing to a larger or smaller scale. You can also use different tools such as photocopying or projecting an image. By drawing or photocopying onto acetate, you can use an overhead projector to project onto a wall. Using large sheets of paper taped to the wall, you can then redraw to a completely new scale. Smaller scale is also possible and is used a lot for putting drawn images into a repeat pattern. It is also possible to reduce or enlarge the detail of drawings through photocopying or scanning onto the computer.

The drawing exercise on pages 140–141 demonstrates how scale can be changed by taping your pencil onto a large stick and drawing on a large sheet of paper on the wall.

12
This student has taken a photograph of a building from an interesting angle and used this as their drawing reference. Careful observation has been used to study the colour and scale captured in the photograph.

13
In this charcoal sketch, a sense of scale has again been achieved through perspective drawing techniques.

13

SCALE-DRAWING EXERCISE

Using an existing drawing, mark out a 10 × 10 cm area masking or covering the rest of the picture. Using just monotone, redraw this area at a scale of 25 × 25 cm and also 4 × 4 cm.

TWO-DIMENSIONAL DRAWING

Two-dimensional drawing refers to a drawing technique whereby only the length and width dimensions are shown. In observational drawing, we are literally 'flattening' a composition, removing any additional information that provides depth and illusion. This can be a very useful technique for design drawing. Drawing from a bird's-eye viewpoint is a good example of how to put this into practice. By observing your composition from a position directly above, you'll notice how the relationship between objects changes. Any shadowing or reflection can be observed as flat.

THREE-DIMENSIONAL DRAWING

Three-dimensional drawing adds the further dimension of depth. This is where perspective, working with light and shade in drawing, adds a three-dimensional quality. Drawing can also be done in three dimensions – paper or a different surface can be cut or manipulated into three-dimensional forms. Describing your subject as a three-dimensional form enables you to consider your composition from a new perspective.

14

14
This student sketchbook shows an example of three-dimensional source material (in this case, tall buildings), translated using paint washes to create a two-dimensional pattern.

15
Simple found materials, such as cardboard packaging, can be used and transformed to create three-dimensional relief patterns as a base on which to draw.

16
Cut cardboard or paper can be used to create simple three-dimensional structures. Experiment with old paperback and hardback books from second-hand shops by cutting through the pages to create different three-dimensional reliefs.

15

16

3D INTO 2D

A useful method for exploring drawing is to transfer from one dimension to another. Using a single sheet of paper, cut, fold and stick it to reshape it into a three-dimensional form. This is now your object for two-dimensional drawing. Using another sheet of the same paper, draw your three-dimensional form in monotone using just line.

Missoni is an Italian fashion house, famed for its use of a wide variety of fabrics in an array of colours and patterns such as stripes, geometrics and florals. They are also well known for their exceptional knitwear collections. The Missoni brand now extends to homeware and 'Hotel Missoni', a lifestyle hotel chain that plans to build and develop hotels across the world.

▶ **17–22**
MISSONI DESIGNS FROM AUTUMN/WINTER 2011

Missoni's 'fairytale' collection for autumn/winter 2011 is inspired by magic and fantasy, 'enchanted and enchanting fairies'. The collection comprises contrasting textiles: ice-cream coloured tweeds and florals, together with patchworked animal skins.

17

18

19

20

21

22

James Donald is principally a handweaver. Current collections of handwoven pieces include scarves that use weave structures based on images created using smart-phone technology. These 'app drawings' have been further developed into stationery, ceramics and jewellery collections, mixing handmade marks and traditional materials with state-of-the-art lasercutting technology. This diversification of his design range is moving James towards developing his own distinctive brand as a creative maker and thinker, strongly influenced by his training as a weaver.

James also co-runs the retail design space Concrete Wardrobe with his business partner Fiona McIntosh, a silkscreen printer. As well as selling their own work, they also sell and promote Scottish-based or trained designer makers and quality craftsmakers' work.

HOW DID YOU GET STARTED?

I started off doing a Higher National Certificate (HNC) and subsequently a Higher National Diploma (HND) in Spatial Design, before completing a degree in Constructed Textiles, specializing in tapestry, weave and printmaking. More recently, I completed a Masters in Design.

WHERE DO YOU WORK?

I work from a large studio complex, which houses 45 studios with 70 designers, craftspeople and artists in the heart of Leith, Edinburgh. My studio houses two looms – one 32-shaft computerized, Dutch-made Louet loom and a Hattersly Domestic, which dates back to the 1930s and hails from the Isle of Harris. The studio also houses my extensive collection of yarns, books and fabrics. I use the studio as a communal space to teach weekend weaving classes.

WHAT IS THE ENVIRONMENT LIKE IN YOUR STUDIO?

I like to think I have created a very colourful and homely atmosphere. The studio has a distinctive smell due to the yarns I use and this always triggers memories for my visitors and students! But while it's homely, it 's also important to point out that it's a working space. I'm very serious about using my time efficiently when I'm in the space.

CAN YOU TELL ME ABOUT YOUR DESIGN PROCESS? HOW DO YOU GENERATE IDEAS?

I have generated a wealth of design ideas from travelling around the Outer Hebrides and the Shetland Islands: drawing, mark-making and photographing the landscape and environment. These images were further recorded and manipulated on an iPhone, using up to four different app processes, and the end results are what I call my 'app drawings'. Sometimes, these 'app drawings' are redrawn using mixed-media techniques and then further developed into a series of treble-cloth woven structures.

I find this method of working both stimulating and rewarding as I now have a huge library of images I can work from and revisit. The 'app drawings' are now being used to produce household items and some are being taken into digital print for fashion.

23

23
One of James Donald's handcrafted woven scarves, as worn by a male model.

24
A section of a double-cloth weave, showing the intricate relief pattern. A hallmark of Donald's design work.

25
A close-up of an open weave, showing the use of light within the design.

24

WHERE DO YOU START YOUR RESEARCH?

I always start with the handmade mark. For me, this is fundamental to my process... to make a mark that I can then blend and manipulate using numerous new technology platforms really excites me creatively.

CAN YOU DESCRIBE YOUR DESIGN PROCESS FROM START TO FINISH?

Key to my design process is communication and an openness to making mistakes. I hate the word 'mistakes' though, and would prefer to talk about 'happy accidents' – understanding why a process works or doesn't work can lead to very exciting developments. I learned this while studying for my Masters and the method has been further honed in subsequent years while making my 'app drawings'.

I enjoy communicating my ideas, thoughts and processes within different situations and to different people. I have never stopped learning and being inquisitive. I'm happy to share my 'secrets', as I believe this is the only true way a sector grows and develops.

WHAT INSPIRES YOU?

My environment and the people that are directly around me. I have worked very hard at developing an open, honest and transparent work ethic where communication is key.

WHAT OR WHO HAS HAD THE MOST INFLUENCE ON YOUR WORK?

My influences are very fluid and I am a bit of a magpie when it comes to collecting the work of others. I currently draw inspiration from ceramicists such as Susan Williams Ellis, John Clappison, Jessica Tait, Lara Scobie and Clare Crouchman.

International travel has also allowed me to meet designers and makers from around the world and I have immense admiration for Reiko Sudo, Junichi Aria, Chiyoko Tanaka (Japan), Liz Williamson, Dani Marti (Australia) and Matthew Harris, Laura Thomas (UK).

WHAT IS YOUR GREATEST ACHIEVEMENT TO DATE?

To still be going since graduating from my degree, making my own work and being my own boss. I am fully aware that it could be 'goodbye Vienna' tomorrow. There have been other successes in my story (as well as disasters) but how we define success is very much an individual paradigm.

DO YOU HAVE ANY ADVICE FOR THOSE THINKING OF A CAREER IN TEXTILE DESIGN?

Don't think of yourself as a single-discipline creative person. Be versatile in your approach to what you do, try everything and don't regret what you have done – rather be glad you had a go and learned from the experience.

Training as a weaver may have shaped me, my development and career path, it may be what I do best but I am more than a weaver ... I weave therefore I am!

25

'Presentation is EVERYTHING.'

ROGER GRIFFITHS

APPENDIX:
HOW TO PRESENT YOUR RESEARCH

Once research has been completed, it needs to be prepared for presentation. This might be for a number of reasons. Your research might need to be presented, for example, for an assessment or for an interview for a course or design job, or simply to update your portfolio. Presentation and effective visual and verbal communication skills are key for every designer.

Preparing to present your work is often the first opportunity to review all the work you have done so far. It is an opportunity to reflect on what you have achieved, a time to consider what to do next and to learn new skills of visually presenting and talking about your work.

1
A photograph of a student's final textile work, using a model to illustrate how a piece might be worn on the body.

Once your research is complete, you will need to select key pieces for presentation that, in your opinion, best represent your abilities and ideas.

Visual presentation is essentially about preparing your work for other people to look at. This can be for an interview, a course or module assessment, a review with tutors and peers or simply a point at which you update your portfolio in the same way that you might update a CV or resumé. It is very important to keep a record and document all areas of your practice – both in written and visual form. If you start this from the outset, it makes life much easier. You might need to present or prepare your work at short notice and having this at least partly prepared can save an enormous amount of time. In time, you will build up a range of information for presentation – visual and written – that enables you to respond effectively to any situation.

WHAT IS A PORTFOLIO?

A portfolio is a body of visual work that represents what you have achieved so far. Your portfolio will contain examples of your most successful work, and will best represent your approach to solving design problems, demonstrating your drawing and visual skills, and your ability to think laterally. A portfolio also includes sketchbooks and notebook work that enables a potential client or course tutor to understand how you solve problems and think through design. Not every piece of work needs to be fully resolved. Your portfolio represents you – make sure that inside and out it reflects this well. It doesn't look professional if you have beautiful creative work in an old scruffy case. When the contents start looking even slightly tatty, make sure that you remount your work.

Your portfolio is contained within a large, flat case suitable for carrying a number of loose sheets of paper. Portfolio cases can be bought in most art supply shops and vary in size from A1 (D) to A4 (A (letter)). You will probably want to start with an A1 (D) or A2 (C) portfolio.

2
An example of a student's inspiration board using photography, drawing and text to tell the story.

Inspiration

falling bits

fragile

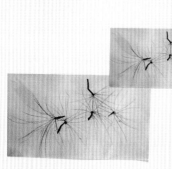
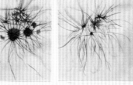

conservation of nature

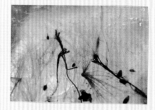

During the drawing week I found a plant in the Botanical Garden which looked magical in the sunshine and inspired me. The falling bits of the plant for me symbolise the fragility of nature and it made me think about how much harm we cause for the planet in these modern years. I used my photographs as a first step to find my colour palette and to get me thinking. I froze some bits of different plants and as a result I got new compositions, forms and pattern. During this project I tried to translate the messages of this plant into fabric.

When I started my research for the context of the outcomes I was looking for lights, transparency and airiness. I didn't make any decisions about the final pieces in terms of whether they should be fashion related or interiors. I think it was a good idea because my outcomes ended up very different so I would use them in very different contexts.

Then I started to draw from my photographs using different materials and techniques. I think I discovered my subject quite fully but I would do it in a very different way if I could start it again. I think I have to make more decisions during the development process mainly about my colour palette but also about the atmosphere I want to achieve. I don't feel there's a strong link between the different pages in my sketchbook, I had so many different ideas but I didn't take the time to discover one of them in depth.

I finally choose a painting from my sketchbook as main inspiration for textiles in practice and I picked up other bits from different designs. So I got my colour palette sorted and I used a combination of bubbles and lines. I think my final pieces turned out to be quite successful in terms of translating my subject but obviously I wasn't familiar enough with the techniques. I also liable to overdo things which was my major problem during the mixed media week. I had to learn how to keep my samples simple and keep them related to my subject. I'm not sure if that week was a big success for me.

Knitting was very different because I know only a couple techniques so I couldn't overdo things. I learned how not to use certain materials like mohair and how to do fully-fashioned shaping. My difficulty during that week was using the knitting machine properly. I have ladders in all of my samples and I couldn't figure it out what causes them. I think I just have to practise more. Apart from that I'm quite happy with my final samples and I can't wait to learn more about knitting.

The print week was very interesting because we learnt a lot of new techniques and I tried to use them all in my samples. I hand painted one of them, I used monoprinting on another and I used the discharger onto a top of a 'sponge painted' one with my screen what we made earlier. I also mixed up my first acid dyes which wasn't a big success at first but I corrected them with the readymade ones in the print room. Next time if I want pale colours I will use much less dye powder to get the right colours so I won't need manutex and water to make them paler.

Although I'm not completely satisfied with my work during this semester I learned a lot about sketchbook work, new techniques and how to present my work.

2

fo·cus (fks)
n. pl. fo·cus·es or fo·ci (-s, -k)
1.
a. A point at which rays of light or other radiation converge or from which they appear to diverge, as after refraction or reflection in an optical system: the focus of a lens. Also called focal point.
b. See focal length.
2.
a. The distinctness or clarity of an image rendered by an optical system.
b. The state of maximum distinctness or clarity of such an image: in focus; out of focus.
c. An apparatus used to adjust the focal length of an optical system in order to make an image distinct or clear: a camera with automatic focus.
3. A center of interest or activity. See Synonyms at center.
4. Close or narrow attention; concentration: "He was forever taken aback by [New York's] pervasive atmosphere of purposefulnessthe tight focus of its drivers, the brisk intensity of its pedestrians" (Anne Tyler).
5. A condition in which something can be clearly apprehended or perceived: couldn't get the problem into focus.
6. Pathology The region of a localized bodily infection or disease.
7. Geology The point of origin of an earthquake.
8. Mathematics A fixed point whose relationship with a directrix determines a conic section.
v. fo·cused or fo·cussed, fo·cus·ing or fo·cus·sing, fo·cus·es or fo·cus·ses
v.tr.
1. To cause (light rays, for example) to converge on or toward a central point; concentrate.
2.
a. To render (an object or image) in clear outline or sharp detail by adjustment of one's vision or an optical device; bring into focus.
b. To adjust (a lens, for example) to produce a clear image.
3. To direct toward a particular point or purpose: focused all their attention on finding a solution to the problem.
v.intr.
1. To converge on or toward a central point of focus; be focused.
2. To adjust one's vision or an optical device so as to render a clear, distinct image.
3. To concentrate attention or energy: a campaign that focused on economic issues.

3
Student presentation board. Note the use of the text as an effective design and communication tool.

3

PRESENTATION BOARDS

Presenting your work essentially means mounting your drawings, inspiration, photographs and any other workings onto boards. The size of board will depend on the size of your piece for mounting and whether you are mounting more than one piece of work together. If possible, you will want to mount your work on the same weight and size of board to keep a uniform, clean and easily 'readable' body of work together. Remember that the board needs to communicate effectively. Keep your mounting simple. Always use a white card unless you can really justify the need for a different colour, for example if your work is predominantly or all-white you will need to contrast this. It is important that the board allows your work to speak for itself without being overly cluttered. Choose either a good quality white cartridge paper or thin white card. The higher the quality of board, the better the work will look, but it doesn't need to be the most expensive! Don't choose a heavy board as you must remember that you will need to be able to carry your portfolio with a number of mounted works!

Float mount onto plain white cartridge paper or thin white board. This means laying your work on top of the board. Do not cut out a frame or box mount. This rarely looks good. Remember to carefully consider where to place your visual research on the board. Always start from the centre. Mark out with a pencil and ruler where you will finally position pieces, making sure that everything is straight. If you are using any text on your board, make sure it is word-processed with a font style and size that is simple, relevant and doesn't overshadow the work.

You can fix your work to the board using either a mounting spray or tape (double-sided or masking). The advantage of using a mounting spray is that you can reposition and remove pieces easily. Be careful where you spray though. Make sure it is in a well-ventilated area. Colleges will often have a specific area for this and will not allow this

to be done anywhere else. Using double-sided tape will enable you to easily move work for presentation elsewhere. Make sure that no tape is showing on the front.

Any work using charcoal, chalk pastels or soft pencils needs to be fixed to prevent smudging. Fixative sprays or aerosols can be used for this purpose but again, this needs to be done in a well-ventilated area. If necessary, you can always place a sheet of white tissue paper over the top to prevent other boards from being marked.

AUTHOR TIP

Mount your work on standard white paper or lightweight card.

If you need to cut paper to size, make sure that it is uniform, square and has clean edges.

If mounting visual research with textiles, do not glue textiles down – they cannot be easily removed or remounted.

Do not smudge spray mount onto photographs – it looks terrible in daylight and collects dust.

4

MOOD/STORYBOARDS

A moodboard or storyboard quite simply
captures your gathered visual stimuli –
photographs, cuttings, colours, textures, patterns.
This might also include examples of fabrics,
yarns or accessories. The rule with moodboards
is that 'anything goes', but they must clearly
communicate a mood or story. The point of the
board is not to formally represent some aspect
of the design, but to simply act as inspiration –
perhaps providing a starting point for a particular
theme or pattern/colour scheme.

4
An example of a student
moodboard bringing drawings,
fashion images and textile
samples together to tell the
story of the work.

5
A selection of work from
Ann Marie Faulkner's final year
collection. Note how the textile
work has been presented together
with photographs of how the
clothing/textiles might be worn.

5

Machine knitted with wire, monofilament and lambswool inside to add interest to tubes.

Knitted tube 2
Hand knitted using a circular needle.

Knitted tube 3
Hand knitted with wire. More organic feel to the tubes.

Wire frame background.

These three samples are ideas on how to link the tubes to the frame.

Manually stitching the wire tubes onto frame.

Making sock heels with lambswool onto a wire background, felting the lambswool and cutting the top off to make a tube.

Casting on a few needles onto the wire and knitting the lambswool onto it.

6

Computer Aided Design (CAD) is increasingly being used as a presentation tool. This is useful for a number of different types of presentation. Work can be photographed or scanned directly onto your computer where aspects of it can then be manipulated. You might want to show different colour variations or changes in size, or you might want to demonstrate how an area of your visual research can create a pattern or a repeat. You may also wish to add text directly onto an image or drawing.

The results will often then be printed out using a colour printer on good quality photographic or print paper for mounting. Sometimes, however, you may be required to send off a CD of your work for a job or college application. In this instance, make sure that your images are of the highest quality resolution (around 300 dpi). Make sure that you save and title your work with your name and order your work to ensure that the external viewer examines each piece in the correct order.

POWERPOINT

Microsoft PowerPoint presentations are now often used to simultaneously show and talk about your work. PowerPoint presentations are in themselves design challenges. The overall look of your PowerPoint presentation needs to reflect your own individual style and present your work as well as possible. Be careful not to be overawed by all the special effects and predesigned templates in a PowerPoint application. They seldom work well for art and design purposes! Keep it simple. Remember; the same rules apply as for your board presentations.

Plan what you are going to say for each slide. Keep simple notes as triggers and try not to read directly from a sheet. Remember that you need to talk to your audience, so engage with them and look at them! By watching others, you will begin to know what works for this type of presentation. Finally,

remember to keep within the time slot that you have been given by making sure that you practice and rehearse beforehand. We will discuss verbal presentation in more depth on pages 164–165.

WEBSITE

The majority of textile designers will have an online presence, whether this is through their own individual website or as a collective group. Many students will start to build their own website from the beginning of their design course. It is helpful to start thinking about this early on as it will give you time to refine and explore what is the best approach for you. This is becoming easily accessible to all – domain names (the website address) are affordable and web design software packages are becoming increasingly user friendly. Blogs and social network sites also provide opportunities for you to present your work externally and to make and receive comments, and to obtain feedback.

6
Your presentation boards can be photographed and then placed onto a CD or used in another digital format. Here, a student's work is highly structured, which can be well presented on screen.

Being able to visually present your work requires one set of skills, whilst talking and articulating your work requires quite another. Many people don't like the idea of talking to an audience. There is, without doubt, often a certain degree of anxiety for everyone in this. Remember that you are not alone! Being able to talk about your work, to express yourself and your ideas is an important skill that you will find you can transfer to other situations throughout your life. It is a skill that we can all learn – practice, planning and plenty of preparation will help to build your confidence.

USING TECHNOLOGY

Working with technology, such as a computer, while talking about your work, can often feel daunting, especially if it's the first time. Always make sure that everything works technically and run through your presentation beforehand. Make sure that you know exactly what you want to say about each slide and be careful to keep within the time allowed.

7
A student presenting and talking about her sketchbook work.

8
Student work on mounted board, demonstrating good consideration of the layout and composition of the work to be presented.

AUTHOR TIP

Look and act like a professional. Everyone will have confidence in what you say.

Make sure that everyone can hear you.

Make eye contact and make sure that you engage with everyone.

Do you need to introduce yourself? Does everyone know who you are?

Always start positively.

Check how long you have available to talk.

Throw away all of your notes and rely on good cues on small hand-held cards instead.

Remember; you know your work better than anyone else.

At the end, ask if there are any questions.

Development

Throughout this book, we have aimed to provide you with the information and skills you need in order to undertake textile research. This has been based on our design and teaching practice. The fundamental techniques for developing research have been discussed and you can now apply these to your own projects. We encourage you to be as creative and experimental as possible so that you can develop your own visual language for design.

It is important to constantly challenge yourself with new media and different drawing and visualization techniques. Over time, your confidence in these areas will grow and you will begin to discover more about yourself as a designer. As a dynamic design discipline, textiles is always evolving. A good designer is constantly excited and inspired by the world around them, searching out new areas to challenge existing perceptions of textile design.

Don't be afraid to make mistakes. Mistakes are at the heart of creative design practice and many designers find that they are the inspiration and driving force for a new body of work.

This book aims to start you on a voyage of discovery where you will learn new insights, skills and knowledge, which will hopefully inspire you to pursue a career within textile design. We wish you all the best in your chosen career and encourage you to enjoy getting there!

1
A digital floral design
by Aimie Bene.

This glossary aims to concisely explain some of the terms used in this book.

ABSTRACT   An idea or concept not based on reality.

AESTHETIC   Refers to the quality and visual appearance of an object or design.

CAMOUFLAGE   A pattern or design that blends into the environment.

COMMERCIAL   Design work specifically aimed at the mass market.

COMMISSIONED   The purchase of a piece of work developed for a specific client or location.

COMPOSITION   The organization of visual elements within a specified area.

COMPUTER-AIDED DESIGN (CAD)
The use of computer technology for the process of design.

CONCEPTUAL   An idea which focuses on meaning as the main driving force.

CONTEMPORARY   Modern and part of the present day.

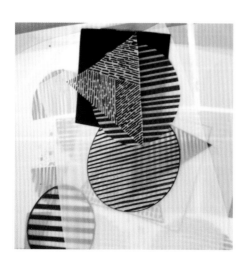

CONTEXTUAL   Refers to information about the users of a design or product.

CRAFT   Creative practices defined either by their relationship to functional or utilitarian products, or by their knowledge and use of traditional and new media.

FORECASTING   The process of predicting what the future will look like.

PALETTE   A group of colours selected to work together.

PATTERN   Decorative forms found in nature, science and art.

PRIMARY SOURCE   Original material or evidence created by the person sourcing the information.

PROJECT BRIEF   Provides the foundation for the start of a project.

MIXED MEDIA   The use of more than one medium.

MOOD BOARDS   A visual presentation that may consist of images, text and samples used to develop design concepts and to communicate ideas to others.

MOTIF   A repeating theme or pattern.

NARRATIVE   A story or a series of events.

REPEAT   An image or motif that recurs.

SENSORY   Relates to the senses of touch, smell, taste, hearing and seeing.

SECONDARY SOURCE   Information that has been presented elsewhere.

SWATCHES   Small pieces of fabric used as an example of a design.

VISUAL LANGUAGE   The method of communicating visual elements.

SUSTAINABILITY   Refers to the long-term maintenance of the environment, society and the economy.

Recommended books

Black S. (ed) 2006. *Fashioning Fabrics: Contemporary Textiles in Fashion.* London: Black Dog Publishing

Blechman H. and Newman A. 2004. *Disruptive Pattern Material: An Encyclopaedia of Camouflage.* London: Firefly Books

Bowles M. and Isaac C. 2009. *Digital Textile Design* (Portfolio Skills). London: Laurence King

Braddock S. E. and O'Mahony M. 1999. *Techno Textiles: Revolutionary fabrics for fashion and design.* London: Thames & Hudson

Braddock S. E. and O'Mahony M. 2005. *Techno Textiles 2: Revolutionary fabrics for fashion and design* (2nd ed). London: Thames & Hudson

Brereton R. 2009. *Sketchbooks: The Hidden Art of Designers, Illustrators and Creatives.* London: Laurence King

Clark S. 2011. *Textile Design* (Portfolio series). London: Laurence King

Colchester C. 2007. *Textiles Today: A Global Survey of Trends and Traditions.* London: Thames & Hudson

Cole D. 2007. *Patterns: New Surface Design.* London: Laurence King

Cole D. 2010. *Textiles Now.* London: Laurence King

Darwent C., MacFarlane K., Stout K. and Kovats T. (eds) 2005. *The Drawing Book: A Survey of Drawing - The Primary Means of Expression.* London: Black Dog Publishing

Fletcher K. 2008. *Sustainable Fashion and Textiles: Design Journeys.* Abingdon: Earthscan

Genders C. 2009. *Pattern, Colour and Form: Creative Approaches by Artists.* London: A&C Black

Greenlees K. 2005. *Creating Sketchbooks for Embroiderers and Textile Artists.* London: Batsford

Grey M. 2008. *Textile Translations: Mixed Media.* Middlesex: D4daisy books

Hedley G. 2010. *Drawn to Stitch: Line, Drawing and Mark-Making in Textile Art.* Loveland, CO: Interweave Press

Hornung D. 2004. *Colour: A Workshop Approach.* London: McGraw-Hill

Jones O. 2001. *The Grammar of Ornament.* Deutsch Press

Juracek J.A. 2002. *Natural Surfaces: Visual Research for Artists, Architects and Designers.* London: WW Norton & Company

Lee R. 2008. *Contemporary Knitting: For Textile Artists.* London: Batsford

Legrand C. 2008. *Textiles: A World Tour: Discovering Traditional Fabrics and Patterns.* London: Thames & Hudson

Lewis G. 2009. *2000 Colour Combinations: For Graphic, Textile and Craft Designers.* London: Batsford

McFadden D. R., Scanlan J. and Edwards J.S. 2007. *Radical Lace and Subversive Knitting.* New York: Museum of Arts & Design

McQuaid M. and McCarty C. 1999. *Structure and Surface: Contemporary Japanese Textiles.* New York: Museum of Modern Art

Meller S. and Elffers J. 2002. *Textile Designs: Two Hundred Years of European and American Patterns Organized by Motif, Style, Color, Layout and Period.* London: Thames & Hudson

Oei L. and De Kegel C. 2008. *The Elements of Design: Rediscovering Colours, Textures, Forms and Shapes.* London: Thames & Hudson

O'Neil P. 2008. *Surfaces and Textures: A Visual Sourcebook.* London: A&C Black

Quinn B. 2009. *Textile Designers at the Cutting Edge.* London: Laurence King

Renshaw L. 2010. *Mixed-Media and Found Materials* (Textiles Handbooks) London: A&C Black

Scott J. 2003. *Textile Perspectives in Mixed-Media Sculpture.* Marlborough: Crowood Press

Sudo K. and Birnbaum A. 1997. *Boro Boro.* Tokyo: Nuno Corporation Books

Sudo K. and Birnbaum A. 1998. *Fuwa Fuwa.* Tokyo: Nuno Corporation Books

Sudo K. and Birnbaum A. 1999. *Kira Kira.* Tokyo: Nuno Corporation Books

Sudo K. and Birnbaum A. 1999. *Shim Jimi.* Tokyo: Nuno Corporation Books

Sudo K. and Birnbaum A. 1997. *Suké Suké.* Tokyo: Nuno Corporation Books

Sudo K. and Birnbaum A. 1999. *Zawa Zawa.* Tokyo: Nuno Corporation Books

Tellier-Loumagne F. 2005. *The Art of Knitting: Inspirational Stitches, Textures and Surfaces.* London: Thames & Hudson

Thittichai K. 2009. *Experimental Textiles: A Journey Through Design, Interpretation and Inspiration.* London: Batsford

Museums

Victoria and Albert Museum (V&A)
Cromwell Road
South Kensington
London
SW7 2RL
London
UK
www.vam.ac.uk

The Fashion & Textile Museum
83 Bermondsey Street
London
SE1 3XF
UK
www.ftmlondon.org

Design Museum
Shad Thames
City of London
SE1 2YD
UK
www.designmuseum.org

Textiel Museum
Goirkestraat 96
5046 GN Tilburg
Netherlands
www.textielmuseum.nl

Musée des Arts décoratifs
Musée des Arts de la mode
et du textile
107 rue de rivoli
75001 Paris
France
www.ucad.fr

Cooper-Hewitt, National Design
Museum
2 East 91st Street
New York, NY 10128
USA
www.cooperhewitt.org

Fashion Institute of Technology
7th Ave & W 27th St
New York, NY 10001
USA
www.fitnyc.edu

Galleries and Open Studios
Contemporary Applied Arts
CAA Gallery
2 Percy Street
London
W1T 1DD
UK
www.caa.org.uk

Gabriel's Wharf
56 Upper Ground
London
SE1 9PP
UK
www.coinstreet.org

Oxo Tower Wharf
Bargehouse Street
South Bank
London
SE1 9PH
UK
www.coinstreet.org

The Scottish Gallery
16 Dundas Street
Edinburgh
EH3 6HZ
UK
www.scottish-gallery.co.uk

Publications and magazines

10

Another Magazine

Bloom

Blueprint

Dazed & Confused

Elle

Elle Decoration

Fibrearts

Frieze

i-D

Issue One

Lula

Marie Claire

Marmalade

Nylon

Selvedge

Tank

Textile Forum

Textile View

View on Colour

Viewpoint

Vogue

Websites

www.newdesigners.com

www.originuk.org

www.100percentdesign.co.uk

www.premierevision.fr

www.pittimmagine.com

www.texi.org

www.craftscouncil.org.uk

www.designcouncil.org.uk

www.embroiderersguild.com

www.etn-net.org

Acknowledgements

We would like to thank everyone who has so generously contributed and supported us during this project. In particular, we would like to thank Marian Ball, Johanna Basford, Rebecca Black, J.R. Campbell, Peta Carling, James Donald, Becky Earley, Carlene Edwards, Ann Marie Faulkner, Malcolm Finnie, Linda Florence, Tim Gresham, Angharad McLaren, Lee Mitchell, Rie NII, at The Kyoto Costume Institute, Sawako Ogitani at Miyake Design Studio, Lucy Orta, Freddie Robins, Alan Shaw, Timorous Beasties, Donna Wilson.

We would also like to thank our past and current students who have provided inspiration and have kindly allowed so many images of their work to illustrate this book. We would like to especially thank Diane Allen, Aimie Bene, Catherine Brunet, Katy Birchall, Laura Cumming, Kirsty Fenton, Carrie Ferguson, Claire Anne Grant, Sara Greenwood, Rachel Haddon, Tarka Heath, Alexandra Hornyik, Connie Lou, Sarah Mitchell, Kirsty Marshall, Serena Quigley, Lucy Robertson, Anna Rzepczynski, Judy Scott, Karen Stewart and Sarah Stewart, Stephanie Szumlakowski.

The publisher would like to thank Jo Horton, Tom Embleton and Bo Breda.

Picture Credits

Cover B. Earley
P 3 Aimie Bene
P 8 Tim Gresham
P 10 Catwalking.com
P 16 Photographer: Yasuaki Yoshinaga Copyright: Miyake Design Studio
P 17 B. Earley
P 18 Studio Shot Image by Alisdair Whyte
PP 22/23 Timorous Beasties
P 24 Catwalking.com
P 27 Judy Scott
P 28 Sudo, Reiko (b.1953): Fabric Mfr. No. 9–133, 1990. New York, Museum of Modern Art (MoMA). Pleated polyester with stainless steel finish 125 × 44 1/2' (317.5 × 113cm). Gift of the manufacturer. Acc. n.: SC445. 1992 ©2011. Digital image, The Museum of Modern Art, New York/ Scala, Florence. ©photo SCALA, Florence.
P 29 Sudo, Reiko (b.1953): Jelly Fish Fabric, 1994. New York, Museum of Modern Art (MoMA). Polyester 251 × 34' (637.5 × 86.4cm). Gift of the manufacturer 120. 1996 ©2011. Digital image, The Museum of Modern Art, New York/Scala, Florence. ©photo SCALA, Florence.
PP 30/31 Donna Wilson
PP 34/35 Judy Scott
P 35 Lucy Robertson
P 36 Judy Scott
P 40 Anna Rzepczynski
PP 43/44 Kirsty Marshall
P 45 Sara Greenwood
PP 46/47 B. Earley
PP 48/49 J.R. Campbell
P 53 Judy Scott
P 55 Judy Scott
P 57 Sara Greenwood
P 65 Maggie Orth
PP 66/67 Copyright Linda Florence
P 72 Courtesy of the artist. Photograph by Douglas Atfield
P 73 Photo John Akehurst, courtesy of the artists
P 74 Judy Scott
P 76 Lucy Robertson
P 79 Karen Stewart
PP 84/85 Catwalking.com
PP 86/88/89 Johanna Basford
P 102 Kirsty Fenton
P 106 Rachel Haddon
P 107 Serena Quigley
P 118 Sarah Stewart
P 122 Sarah Mitchell
P 128 Carlene Edwards

PP 130/131 Image © the artist and courtesy of the artist and Stephen Friedman Gallery, London
PP 132/133 Tim Gresham
P 134 Katy Birchall
P 135 Alexandra Hornyik
P 136 Anna Rzepczynski
P 138 Sara Greenwood
P 139 Judy Scott
P 141 Judy Scott
P 144 Sara Greenwood
P 146 Sara Greenwood
P 147 Anna Rzepczynski
P 148 Sara Greenwood
P 150 Sara Greenwood
PP 152/153 Catwalking.com
PP 154/155 Images by Shannon Tofts and James Donald
P 156 Laura Cumming
P 159 Alexandra Hornyik
P 160 Claire Anne Grant
P 162 Tarka Heath
P 163 Ann Marie Faulkner
P 164 Connie Lou
P 167 Kirsty Marshall
P 169 Aimie Bene

BASICS
TEXTILE DESIGN

Working with ethics

Lynne Elvins
Naomi Goulder

Publisher's note

The subject of ethics is not new, yet its consideration within the applied visual arts is perhaps not as prevalent as it might be. Our aim here is to help a new generation of students, educators and practitioners find a methodology for structuring their thoughts and reflections in this vital area.

AVA Publishing hopes that these **Working with ethics** pages provide a platform for consideration and a flexible method for incorporating ethical concerns in the work of educators, students and professionals. Our approach consists of four parts:

The **introduction** is intended to be an accessible snapshot of the ethical landscape, both in terms of historical development and current dominant themes.

The **framework** positions ethical consideration into four areas and poses questions about the practical implications that might occur. Marking your response to each of these questions on the scale shown will allow your reactions to be further explored by comparison.

The **case study** sets out a real project and then poses some ethical questions for further consideration. This is a focus point for a debate rather than a critical analysis so there are no predetermined right or wrong answers.

A selection of **further reading** for you to consider areas of particular interest in more detail.

Introduction

Ethics is a complex subject that interlaces the idea of responsibilities to society with a wide range of considerations relevant to the character and happiness of the individual. It concerns virtues of compassion, loyalty and strength, but also of confidence, imagination, humour and optimism. As introduced in ancient Greek philosophy, the fundamental ethical question is: *what should I do?* How we might pursue a 'good' life not only raises moral concerns about the effects of our actions on others, but also personal concerns about our own integrity.

In modern times the most important and controversial questions in ethics have been the moral ones. With growing populations and improvements in mobility and communications, it is not surprising that considerations about how to structure our lives together on the planet should come to the forefront. For visual artists and communicators, it should be no surprise that these considerations will enter into the creative process.

Some ethical considerations are already enshrined in government laws and regulations or in professional codes of conduct. For example, plagiarism and breaches of confidentiality can be punishable offences. Legislation in various nations makes it unlawful to exclude people with disabilities from accessing information or spaces. The trade of ivory as a material has been banned in many countries. In these cases, a clear line has been drawn under what is unacceptable.

But most ethical matters remain open to debate, among experts and lay-people alike, and in the end we have to make our own choices on the basis of our own guiding principles or values. Is it more ethical to work for a charity than for a commercial company? Is it unethical to create something that others find ugly or offensive?

Specific questions such as these may lead to other questions that are more abstract. For example, is it only effects on humans (and what they care about) that are important, or might effects on the natural world require attention too?

Is promoting ethical consequences justified even when it requires ethical sacrifices along the way? Must there be a single unifying theory of ethics (such as the Utilitarian thesis that the right course of action is always the one that leads to the greatest happiness of the greatest number), or might there always be many different ethical values that pull a person in various directions?

As we enter into ethical debate and engage with these dilemmas on a personal and professional level, we may change our views or change our view of others. The real test though is whether, as we reflect on these matters, we change the way we act as well as the way we think. Socrates, the 'father' of philosophy, proposed that people will naturally do 'good' if they know what is right. But this point might only lead us to yet another question: *how do we know what is right?*

You
What are your ethical beliefs?

Central to everything you do will be your attitude to people and issues around you. For some people, their ethics are an active part of the decisions they make every day as a consumer, a voter or a working professional. Others may think about ethics very little and yet this does not automatically make them unethical. Personal beliefs, lifestyle, politics, nationality, religion, gender, class or education can all influence your ethical viewpoint.

Using the scale, where would you place yourself? What do you take into account to make your decision? Compare results with your friends or colleagues.

Your client
What are your terms?

Working relationships are central to whether ethics can be embedded into a project, and your conduct on a day-to-day basis is a demonstration of your professional ethics. The decision with the biggest impact is whom you choose to work with in the first place. Cigarette companies or arms traders are often-cited examples when talking about where a line might be drawn, but rarely are real situations so extreme. At what point might you turn down a project on ethical grounds and how much does the reality of having to earn a living affect your ability to choose?

Using the scale, where would you place a project? How does this compare to your personal ethical level?

01 02 03 04 05 06 07 08 09 10

01 02 03 04 05 06 07 08 09 10

Your specifications
What are the impacts of
your materials?

In relatively recent times, we are learning
that many natural materials are in
short supply. At the same time, we are
increasingly aware that some man-made
materials can have harmful, long-term
effects on people or the planet. How much
do you know about the materials that
you use? Do you know where they come
from, how far they travel and under what
conditions they are obtained? When your
creation is no longer needed, will it be
easy and safe to recycle? Will it disappear
without a trace? Are these considerations
your responsibility or are they out of
your hands?

Using the scale, mark how ethical
your material choices are.

Your creation
What is the purpose of your work?

Between you, your colleagues and an
agreed brief, what will your creation
achieve? What purpose will it have in
society and will it make a positive
contribution? Should your work result in
more than commercial success or industry
awards? Might your creation help save
lives, educate, protect or inspire? Form
and function are two established aspects
of judging a creation, but there is little
consensus on the obligations of visual
artists and communicators toward society,
or the role they might have in solving
social or environmental problems.
If you want recognition for being the
creator, how responsible are you for
what you create and where might that
responsibility end?

Using the scale, mark how ethical the
purpose of your work is.

01 02 03 04 05 06 07 08 09 10

01 02 03 04 05 06 07 08 09 10

One aspect of textile design that raises an ethical dilemma is in preserving the cultural traditions of small communities. Woven or handcrafted fabrics and garments can become valuable and highly prized purchases for wealthy collectors, tourists or museums. But this may not provide the community with the continuous flow of income necessary to sustain its needs. Old traditions and styles are being exchanged for more efficient, modern techniques. Commercial pressure to focus on simple designs that are easier to produce in quantity rather than quality pieces that require creativity and complexity is increasingly common. Young people are moving away from small communities and so the knowledge is no longer passed down from generation to generation. How much responsibility should a textile designer take if they want to draw inspiration from traditional designs or techniques? Even if designers wish to prevent the disappearance of traditional methods, what might they most usefully do?

Denim was produced as early as the sixteenth century using a twill weave with un-dyed weft yarn and coloured warp, which created the distinctive diagonal ribbing in the fabric. It was worn by workers because of its strength and durability. The term 'jeans' is said to originate from *Bleu de Genes*, meaning blue material from Genoa, Italy. Baggy denim became the uniform of choice for Genoese sailors and fishermen.

Synonymous with denim, indigo dye has become one of the most important commercial colourants because of the demand for jeans. It was originally derived from plants that were known for their ability to colour fabrics a deep blue. But the natural extraction process was expensive and could not produce the mass quantities required for the expanding market. In 1883, Adolf von Baeyer researched indigo's chemical structure and produced the first commercial production of the synthetic dye for which he received the Nobel Prize in 1905. In more recent years, the synthetic-dye industry has increased environmental standards to reduce the impacts of toxic waste from dye processes. However, there are still companies that flout regulations.

As the world's most popular fibre, cotton farming accounts for around ten per cent of worldwide pesticide use. Although the market for organic pesticide-free cotton is growing, it still represents less than one per cent of global trade. Cotton production also consumes huge quantities of water. In 2007, the Levi Strauss company began assessing the environmental impacts of their 501 jeans and found that more than 3,000 litres of water were used during the complete product cycle. Of this, 49 per cent was used to grow the cotton, 45 per cent is used when people wash their jeans at home and the remaining six per cent is used during the manufacturing process. As a result of their findings, the company is now working on a 'Water<Less' jeans project.

According to Mintel, in 2007, three pairs of jeans were sold every second of every day in Great Britain; with imports totaling approximately 86 million pairs. In a global survey, more than six out of ten people said they love or enjoy wearing denim.

Does the global expansion of a market always represent success?

Is it more ethical to use natural rather than synthetic dyes?

Would you buy a pair of fair trade cotton and organic jeans from an alternative brand, one which has certified ethical standards as an essential part of their operations, as opposed to a market-leading brand?

I wish I had invented blue jeans. They have expression, modesty, sex appeal, simplicity – all I hope for in my clothes.

Yves Saint Laurent

Further reading

AIGA
Design Business and Ethics
2007, AIGA

Eaton, Marcia Muelder
Aesthetics and the Good Life
1989, Associated University Press

Ellison, David
Ethics and Aesthetics in European Modernist Literature:
From the Sublime to the Uncanny
2001, Cambridge University Press

Fenner, David E W (Ed)
Ethics and the Arts:
An Anthology
1995, Garland Reference Library of Social Science

Gini, Al and Marcoux, Alexei M
Case Studies in Business Ethics
2005, Prentice Hall

McDonough, William and Braungart, Michael
Cradle to Cradle:
Remaking the Way We Make Things
2002, North Point Press

Papanek, Victor
Design for the Real World:
Making to Measure
1972, Thames & Hudson

United Nations Global Compact
The Ten Principles
www.unglobalcompact.org/AboutTheGC/TheTenPrinciples/index.html